MAKING SPACE
—DESIGN FOR COMPACT LIVING—

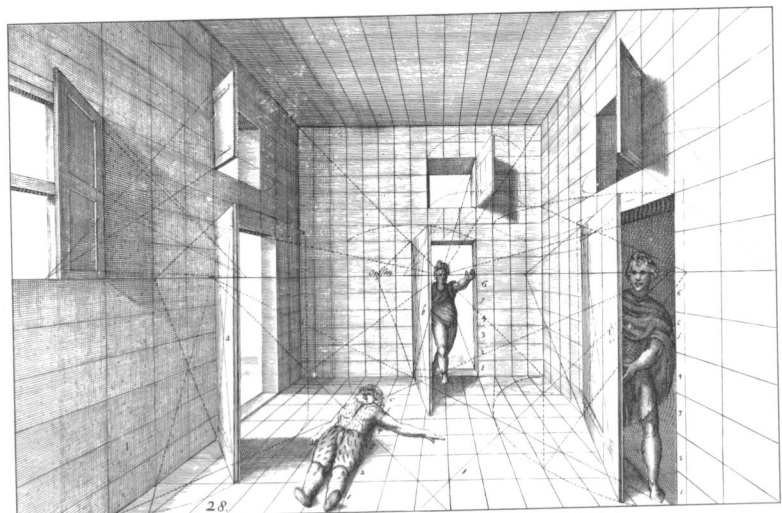

THE OVERLOOK PRESS · WOODSTOCK, NY

MAKING SPACE

DESIGN FOR COMPACT LIVING

RICK BALL

First published in 1989 by

The Overlook Press
Lewis Hollow Road
Woodstock, New York 12498

Library of Congress Cataloging-in-Publication Data

Ball, Richard, 1947–
    Making space:design for compact living/Rick Ball.
        p.   cm.
    Includes index
        1. Room layout (Dwellings). 2. Interior decoration. 3. Personal
    space. 4. Space (Architecture). I. Title.
    NK2113.B35 1989
    728—dc19   88-22431

            ISBN 0-87951-343-8 (cloth)
            ISBN 0-87951-365-9 (paper)

Designed by Peter Campbell

CONTENTS

MAKING SPACE

Living spaces are shrinking, as prices and populations rise. The special problems and opportunities of life in a small space affect an ever-growing number of people – the couple setting up together for the first time on a limited budget and in an expensive city, the old person leaving the large old family house to move into a small retirement home or to share a son's or daughter's house, the working man or woman who needs to fit a darkroom or an office into a packed apartment, single people preferring a small city-centre apartment to a large one in the suburbs, or the growing family who must pack more people into the same number of rooms.

Making Space is a manual of practical design ideas to make living in small spaces less awkward, whether the problem is lack of privacy, an inadequate kitchen or bathroom, or the eternal shortage of storage space.

The problem is basically one of interior design, and the work of some of the world's most interesting specialist professional designers is analysed and illustrated in the following pages. However, the research for this book has proved to us that you don't have to be a professional interior designer to design your interior successfully. We are surrounded by design ideas, and ideas are free.

Experience has led vast numbers of non-professionals to inventive low-cost solutions to the problems of life in a tiny home. Careful planning helps them live the cramped life without learning to loathe either their homes or the people they live with. Many of the most interesting ideas come from people living on the move, in conditions where space economy is crucial. The layout of space and the design of fittings in canal boats, aircraft, submarines, caravans, tents, space shuttles, even prisons, not only illustrate the needs and problems of occupants of a confined space but also provide a large number of ideas adaptable for use at home.

Some non-nomadic cultures are

adept at adapting the tiniest of spaces to elegant living. The traditional Japanese interior is a clear and useful example, where the spaces are flexible, the furniture low and the number of possessions limited.

Even the Japanese tea master might be in awe of St Simeon the Stylite, who could dispute with Diogenes in his barrel the claim to be the patron of people living in small spaces. St Simeon found life in fifth-century Syrian hermitages and monasteries too opulent, and he therefore became the first of the great 'pillar ascetics'. In 423 he moved to a pillar and stayed there for over thirty years, living on a 12ft (3.6m) square platform 60ft (18m) from the ground. He became quite a tourist attraction at the time and inspired a curious fashion for platform living.

Our only tribute to the admirable St Simeon is the platform bed, which is one of the many space-saving ideas examined in *Making Space* as part of our step-by-step invasion of a small space. The book contains practical information to help you make a thorough structural survey of your living space, and there are detailed instructions on producing simple but adequate working drawings or models. These are useful tools when you begin to plan the best use of the space.

Beyond the building stage, we look at the exploitation of decorative devices to make your small space seem bigger than it is. The choice of suitable furniture and appliances will also have an impact on the efficient use of space. Some of the best miniature equipment from manufacturers and designers around

The flat on the left is a one-room living and working space in London. It contains a built-in bed and shelving, classic modern and antique furniture, paintings, books and the tools of bookbinding, scholarship and cooking (see page 91). It is home for three people, who prove that living in a small space does not exclude possessions and pastimes. On the other hand it does mean that furnishings and floor coverings – which are used heavily – must be chosen with care. An elegant solution may not be tough enough, a sad fact proved by the cabin designed in 1935 for Air France by the architect Mallet-Stevens (above). The passengers sat on wicker chairs – elegant, light and resilient enough to be useful in small domestic spaces, airships and ocean liners. They did not, alas, stand up to the acceleration and constant vibration of the aircraft. The seating, lighting and storage systems on today's aircraft can provide ideas relevant to small-space living.

the world is illustrated, along with some of the most absurd.

We are not claiming that small is beautiful in the housing field. It can be very depressing. Yet there are real advantages to small-space living. Small rooms are normally easier and cheaper to heat than large ones; there is less to clean and maintain, and you can save money by being unable to buy more appliances simply because there is no room for them. There is also a certain attraction in the miniature, from dolls' houses, ships in bottles and bonsai trees to toy poodles and the Sony Walkman.

Probably the most important lesson to be learned from the travellers and professional designers is to be aware of yourself and the way you live. The most underused small space of all, we are often told, is the human brain. It can be interesting and profitable to fire up a few brain cells on your design problem, and no one stands more chance of getting it right than you do. The whole point of designing and decorating your own space is to end up with a result that works for you and that you like living with. It doesn't matter if your ideas would not be awarded the design professionals' seal of approval: they do not have to live there.

The ideas in *Making Space* are particularly relevant to people in compact spaces, both those who own their own place and those trying to make the best of a rented apartment filled with the landlord's random selection of junk furniture. Many of the ideas will be useful even if you live in a vast hangar — we all want more room, and *Making Space* will help you find it.

Looking at people forced to live in extremely cramped conditions, where privacy is minimal, can provide both warnings and lessons for anyone planning a small living space, particularly if that space must be shared with others. In Britain's overcrowded prisons, which house the highest number of prisoners per head of population in western Europe, serious unrest has been depressingly common. Many who work in the system are convinced that overcrowding is partly to blame.

Although long-term prisoners will probably have a cell to themselves, which they can decorate to their taste, short-term prisoners and those awaiting trial could be forced to share their cell with two others. In such conditions a pair of bunks along one long wall would face a single bed opposite. For twenty-three hours a day the three men could be locked up with no privacy except inside the earplug of a personal radio. Significantly, the personal stereo cassette player has become an almost essential part of the modern submariner's kit, a simple way of shutting out the rest of the world.

Some find the lack of privacy intolerable, although prisoners from overcrowded home backgrounds predictably find it less stressful. Perhaps the most onerous element in the lack of privacy is the bucket in the cell corner, a w c which the three men must share from about 4:30 in the afternoon until the cell is opened at 7:30 the following morning.

The only ventilation is through a small window in the outside wall. A

There is just enough room to stretch your arms for a body search in prison (above), a luxury the submariner (below) must do without as he tries to clean himself in the 'O' Class diesel-electric boat's cramped shower.

The Boeing 747 seating plan (above, right) and the engraving (below, right) used by William Wilberforce in his anti-slavery campaign show how little the geometry of transatlantic travel has changed.

night in a prison cell would convince anyone of the need for adequate ventilation and opening windows in the smallest of spaces.

Many prisoners deal with the overcrowding by complete withdrawal into themselves, lying on their beds all day without communicating. Rehabilitation workers have found that such people find it hard to wake up once the prison nightmare is over and cannot readjust to life outside.

Each prisoner has a small cupboard for possessions – a few letters, perhaps a change of clothes, a towel, a toothbrush, a plastic knife and fork, metal plates and maybe half a dozen books. There is also a single table and chair which one prisoner may use at breakfast time and all may use to write letters. Pictures can be displayed on the pinboard on the wall.

In certain respects life on a submarine is similar to being in a short-term prison. On a diesel-electric boat the submariner is enclosed with some seventy others for weeks on end. A nuclear submarine will simply stay submerged until the food runs out. As in the prison, privacy is minimal. All the living and working spaces in the boat are linked by a single narrow corridor, in which two people cannot pass with ease. Three tiers of bunks are ranged along one side of the corridor, where the ratings sleep as submarine life passes by. They can at least draw curtains across their bunk for an illusion of privacy.

In the officers' wardroom conditions are sightly better but still

8

very cramped, with eight officers sharing a small room which serves as living-room, office and bedroom. Not surprisingly, caravan designers have been called in to make maximum use of the minimal space. Submariners often complain that the people who design their living spaces rarely have to go to sea in them. Only by living in a space can you decide what is really necessary and genuinely convenient. Not all folding furniture works well, for example. When the boat goes in for a refit, the wardroom makes practical suggestions for improvements, and these are routinely incorporated in the design.

The overcrowding makes for inefficient work. A day's paperwork in the submarine could be finished in a morning in a civilian office. The office desk is also the dining table, with two of the beds serving as seats, supplemented by locker seats similar to piano stools for file stores.

Storage space is everywhere – in the beds, under the mattresses, behind the lights and behind panels in the ceiling and walls. The furniture, from drop-down beds to the refrigerator, is all built in, as are the all-important television monitor, VCR and a cassette tape player. Car cassette players have been used successfully in submarines, as they are small, robust and designed for easy fitting. Cassette tapes tend to wander around the boat, as most people own and use a personal stereo set, but the tapes always come back to their owner. The crowded conditions lead to a sense of community – 'family' is a common description of the atmosphere.

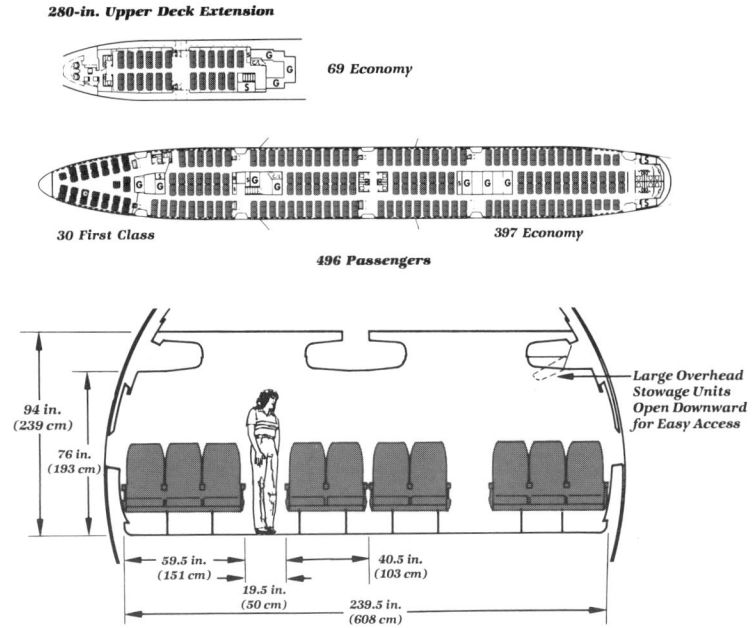

280-in. Upper Deck Extension

69 Economy

30 First Class   397 Economy

496 Passengers

94 in. (239 cm)
76 in. (193 cm)

Large Overhead Stowage Units Open Downward for Easy Access

59.5 in. (151 cm)   40.5 in. (103 cm)
19.5 in. (50 cm)
239.5 in. (608 cm)

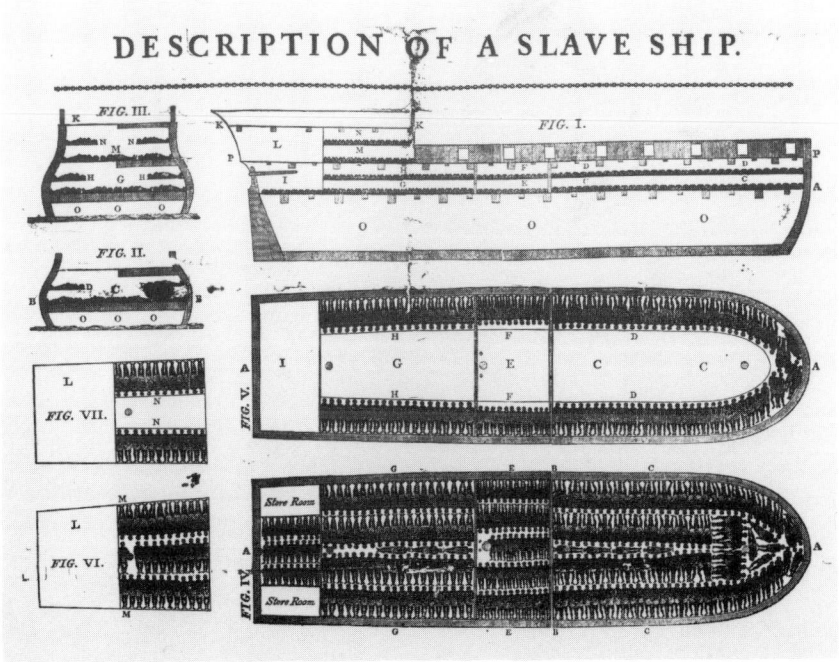

DESCRIPTION OF A SLAVE SHIP.

HOW SMALL IS TOO SMALL?

In New York City, pressures on limited living space conspire to make a mockery of attempts to impose legal minima. A 1986 city report revealed that over 35,000 families were living doubled up illegally, usually with relatives or friends, in apartments owned by the New York City Housing Authority. Groups concerned with the city's housing problems calculated that an additional 45,000 to 200,000 people are forced to live in overcrowded private apartments, envied only by the 60,000 to 80,000 New Yorkers estimated by the National Coalition on the Homeless to be without shelter in the city.

The history of small-space design in New York is dominated by the apartment. Just as London's public housing became smaller after the First World War, so room sizes in New York apartments shrank after the Second World War, when land and construction costs skyrocketed. The New York apartment plans shown on page 13 reflect such major social changes as the virtual disappearance of the servant. This meant more than the simple disappearance of servants' quarters. With no servants, the kitchen now had to move closer to the eating area, for the occupiers' convenience. As time went by, the dining room becomes smaller, moving into an alcove or simply vanishing from the plan. Today even such luxury co-op apartments as those designed by Skidmore Owings and Merrill at Olympic Tower, on 51st Street and Fifth Avenue, are built without dining rooms.

New York City building law defines an apartment as one room that is at least 132sq. ft (12.3sq. m), and a bath. Such minimalist apartments are all too common these days. Meanwhile, uniformity increases. In the famous Dakota, for instance, completed in 1884 on Central Park West, practically every apartment has its own unique floor plan, an almost unthinkable extravagance today. By modern standards most of New York's old apartments are full of 'wasted' space between rooms.

One of the most interesting developments in New York was the early twentieth-century fashion for the so-called artist's studio, which boasted a double-height living room reminiscent of the classic artist's atelier. Artists in fact rarely occupied them. The Hotel des Artistes (1916) on West 67th Street is probably the most famous of the group. Originally the Hotel des Artistes had a common kitchen in the basement where meals were prepared, to be

The multi-storey kennel (left) designed by Walter Ford in 1874 relies on an unusually tolerant collection of dogs, yet it seems less of a fantasy than the famous Japanese capsule hotel (right). If you are willing to bed down in cubicle 4069 the space you save in overcrowded Japan saves you money. It is cheaper than a normal hotel room, cheaper even than the late-night taxi to the suburbs, though the massed smells and snores of an entire cell block can spoil your sleep, in spite of the air conditioning – there is, of course, television to entertain you. Privacy is minimal, and in the morning you will have to share a washroom with many of your fellow guests. It probably works better in Japan, which has a long tradition of public bathing, than it would in the west.

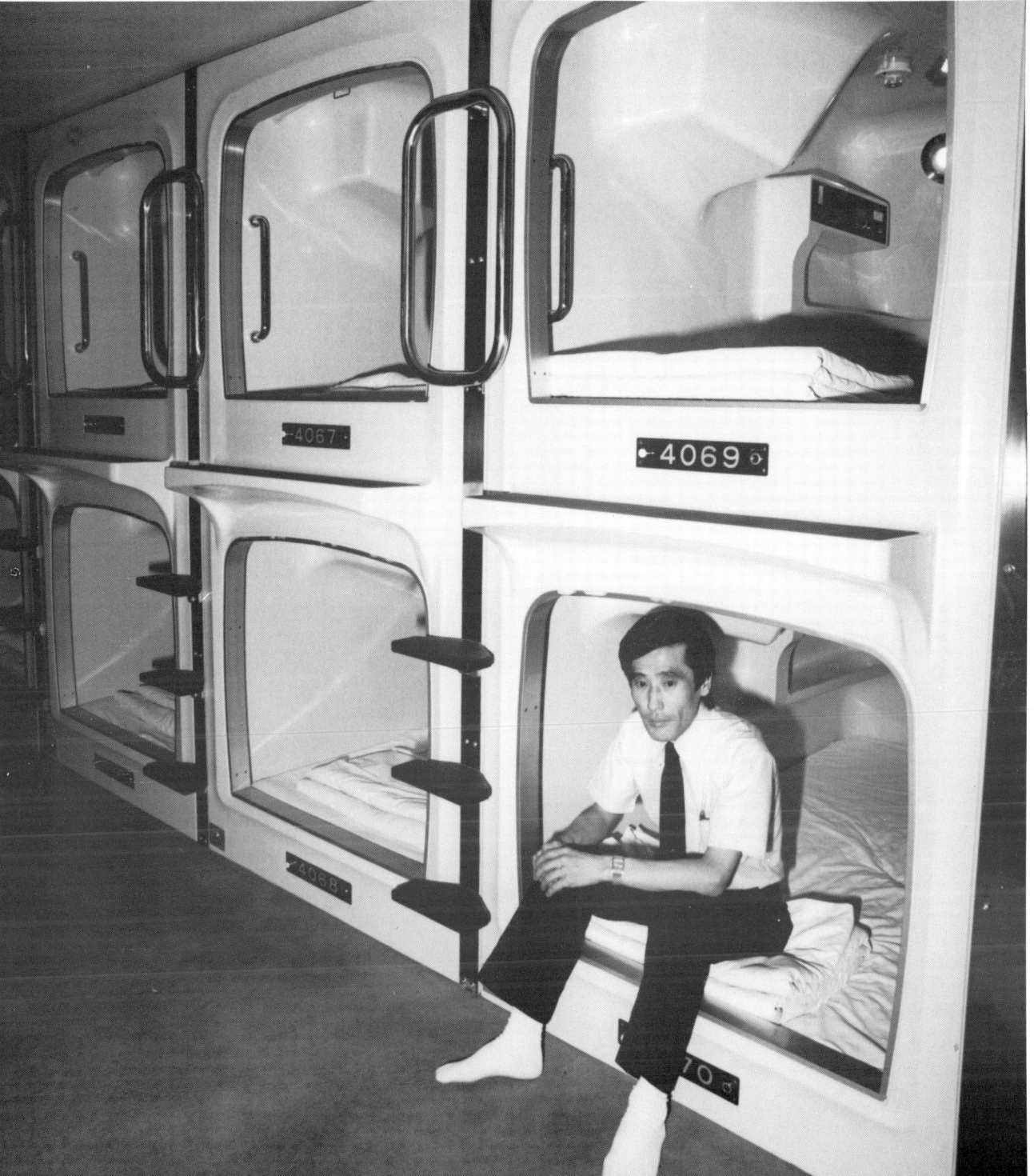

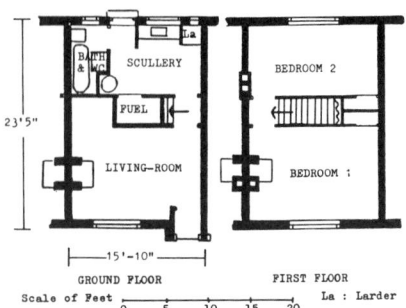

GROUND FLOOR   FIRST FLOOR
Scale of Feet   La : Larder
0   5   10   15   20

Despite the slogan 'homes fit for heroes', post-1918 housing authorities still wanted more units for less money, as this 1922 plan (above) shows. The rooms are tiny, but the big differences between this plan and bottom-of-the-market housing in the 1980s (the replacement of larder and fuel store by fridge and radiators for example) are in services rather than the gross amount of space allowed. Hellman's protest (right) at the way neat diagrams can be used to hide intolerable conditions appeared in the Architect's Journal. *The style he is parodying can be checked out on pages 99 and 107.*

delivered to the hungry apartment dweller above via a dumb-waiter rising through the floors. Problems arose when those on the upper floors regularly found their food intercepted by the occupants on lower floors. This amenity had to be abandoned.

Typically these studio apartments had a high living room overlooked by a balcony, with other rooms squeezed around the main room's perimeter on both levels. In some layouts, one entered the apartment, grandly, on the upper mezzanine level.

The foyer apartment, popular in the 1920s and 1930s, was organized,

as its name implies, around a central foyer. Even today, these foyer apartments often feel modern in their concern to make each room seem like an interlocking part of the whole apartment rather than a completely separate box, which is so often the case in the corridor or railroad apartment.

Overcrowding is a bad thing; everyone agrees about that. Yet the word remains extremely hard to define in square feet or meters. The U.S. Department of Agriculture has laid down guidelines for the country's caged birds, who must be able to extend their wings comfortably within their living space. This seems ungenerous. Space allowances for dogs under the U.S. Animal Welfare Act of 1956 and

1976 are not much more in keeping with a nation supposedly of animal lovers. The kenneled dog must be able to stand up and lie down comfortably. The rules are more specific for the transporting of animals: small dogs must be given a cage with a floor area of at least 1.83 sq. ft (.017 sq. m), large dogs 7.58 sq. ft (.07 sq. m).

Laws also cover people in spaces. Each British office worker, for example, should have at least 40 sq. ft (3.7 sq. m) of floor space and 400 cu. ft (11.3 cu. m) of air to breathe in. Below these limits, the workers are officially overcrowded.

Overcrowding in British homes as defined by the Housing Act of 1985 appears to be considered something of a moral issue, since there is a great

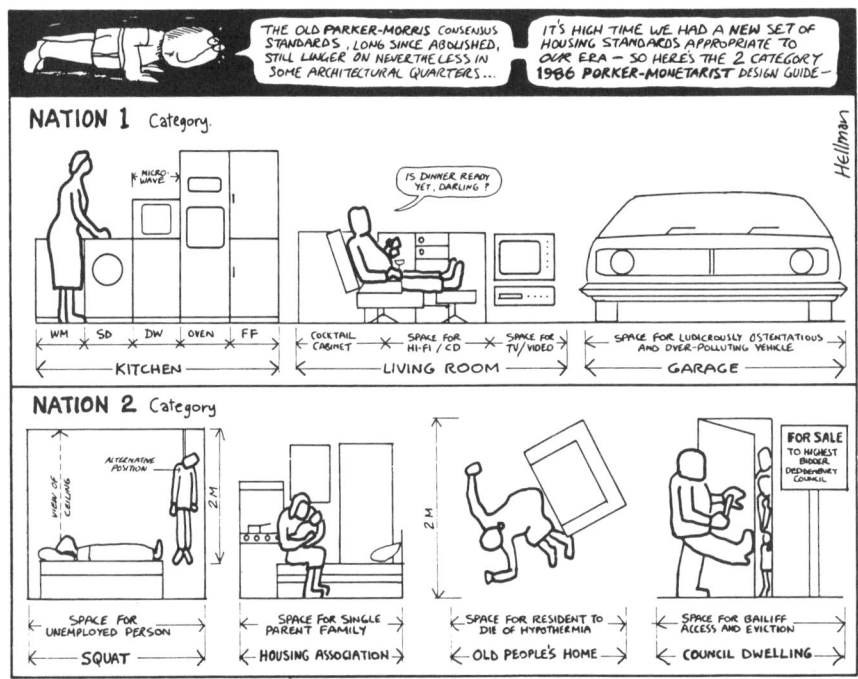

concern about sexual overcrowding. This is said to occur when two people of opposite sexes, over ten years old and not living together as a couple, are forced by a lack of space to sleep in the same room. Small-space designers should bear this in mind. Privacy matters.

In New York City also, building laws specify a 'permitted number' of residents for a dwelling: no room may sleep more than two adults, and habitable rooms must contain at least 400cu. ft (11.3cu. m) of air for each adult, 200cu. ft (5.7cu. m) for each child. Dining bays smaller than 55sq. ft (5.1sq. m), kitchens smaller than 59 sq. ft (5.5sq. m), bathrooms, and lavatories do not count as habitable rooms, and children under two years old are not counted. Those under thirteen years old are considered half a person. This suggests that up to four children may inhabit a room, accompanied, one might suppose, by any number of infants.

The United States' Uniform Building Code, which has been adopted in full by some states and modified by others, gives some interesting minimum standards. These can be useful guidelines for anyone planning to divide up a small space. A studio, or efficiency apartment, for example, should be at least 220sq. ft (20.4sq. m) in floor area, and it must contain a bathroom, a kitchen sink, and refrigerator hook-up, although cooking facitlies are not required. Any studio that houses more than two peole must contain an additional 100sq. ft (9.3sq. m) of floor space for each additional person.

The shrinking New York apartment. These two luxury studio apartments were built in 1929 and 1963. Even if you realize that it was designed for at least two people and had a servant's room, the 1929 version is clearly more spacious. Financial pressure applies at all levels of the market. Paul Goldberger, writing in the New York Times, *points out the odd contradiction that bedrooms have got smaller, but big beds and built-in furniture are commoner: the walls really are moving in on us.*

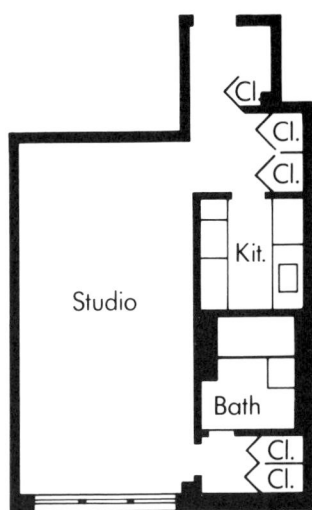

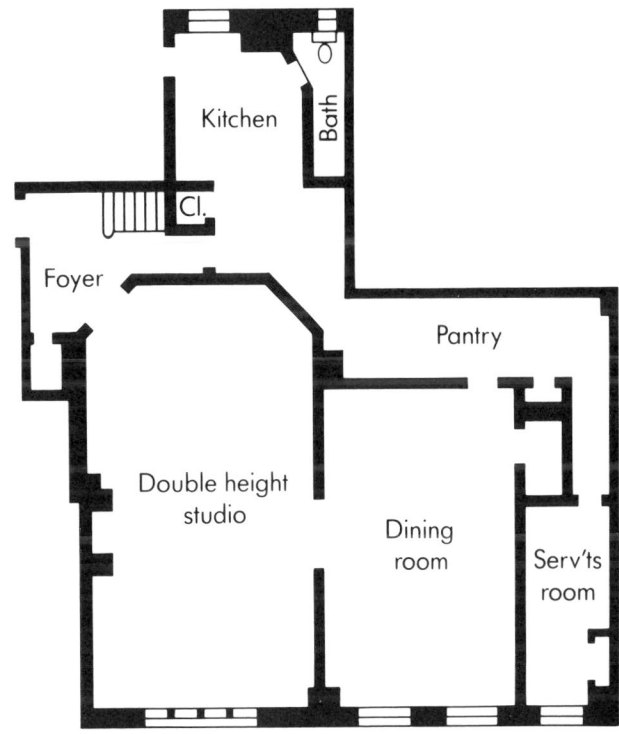

HOW SMALL IS TOO SMALL?

Where an apartment has at least two rooms, the kitchen must be over 50sq. ft (4.7sq. m) in floor area. Bedrooms need be no more than 70sq. ft (6.5sq. m), as long as one room is at least 120sq. ft (11.2sq. m). And all habitable rooms must be at least 7 ft (2.1m) wide.

Windows in all bedrooms and living rooms must be at least one tenth of the floor area in each room and at least 12sq. ft (1.1sq m)—a regulation that can often affect plans to divide a space up by partition walls. In New York City, you cannot partition a room unless each part has at least one window and 70sq. ft (6.5sq. m) of space.

Rooms that are not required to have windows must have adequate artificial lighting. Kitchens without windows must have a mechanical ventilation system, which in New York City should generate six air changes every hour.

New Yorkers must also provide at least one toilet for the first four rooms and one for every seven rooms thereafter, which sounds like a nightmare in the morning rush. The Uniform Building Code outlines a minimum bathrooms size of 5 × 7 ft (1.5 × 2.1m), and the New York City building laws specify a width of at least 28in (710mm) for each toilet. Each apartment, according to the code, must have its own cold drinking water supply and a hot and cold water supply to a basin or sink, which seems very sensible, as does the ruling that every bedroom and living room must be centrally heated. New York City landlords are also required to provide heat between October 1st and May 31st.

Agnes Toward, shorthand typist, died in 1975 at the age of 89. The Glasgow tenement (plan and photograph, below right) at 145 Buccleuch Street into which she and her mother moved in 1911 and from which she discarded little, is now a museum. Although small by modern standards, the flat, built in 1892, would have seemed luxuriously vast to the many families who lived in Glasgow's 'single ends', crammed into a flat no bigger than Miss Toward's kitchen. The kitchen is the most cheerful room in the flat and, because of the massive coal-burning range, was no doubt the warmest. The kitchen range provided hot water, as well as cooking facilities. There was a fixed wringer by the sink, and ironing was done on the kitchen table – irons were heated on the range. The layout is compact, and proves that some solutions really are the natural ones, whether your fuel is taken (as Miss Toward's was) from a coal bunker (hers held five hundredweights) or a power point. The tenement's kitchen and bathroom – a rare feature in 1892 – are on the right of the oddly spacious entrance hall; on the left are the bedroom and parlour, where guests would be entertained on special occasions. Even in the tiny two-roomed Scottish 'but and ben', one room would be kept as 'best' and rarely used, however great the pressure on space. One remarkable feature of both kitchen and parlour is the box bed in an alcove, over which curtains could be drawn during the day. Such box beds – a Glasgow speciality – were barred as unhealthy after 1900. One modern substitute would be a platform bed, like those on pages 91 and 95, if there was space, or something like the bed-settee of the Isokon flat. Neither, one can be sure, would have appealed to Miss Toward.

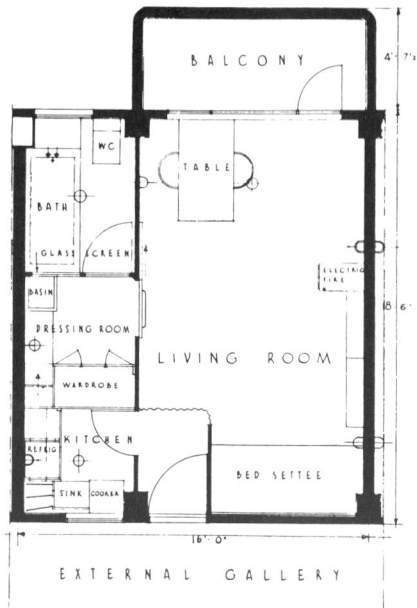

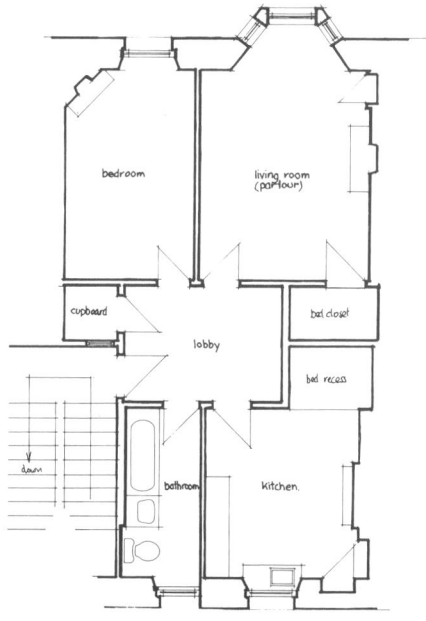

Isokon Flats, built in Hampstead, London, in 1933, were designed by Wells Coates for single professional people. Everything is packed into 275sq. ft (25.5sq. m). A glass screen divides the dressing-room from the bathroom, and the bed doubles as a settee. The tenant could read, sleep or listen to the wireless, but the limited storage and working space assume that she or he will accumulate few possessions. In the photograph (above) of an exhibition mock-up, the removal of a wall exaggerates the apparent size (see plan, opposite above). Blocks of flats like this one were the model for many features in the council flats of the fifties and sixties. In many ways they assume a narrower kind of life than the Glasgow tenement.

HOW SMALL IS TOO SMALL?

Although not all loft beds create rooms in the space above and below, anyone considering building a bed platform should remember that under the Uniform Building Code, all rooms must have a minimum ceiling height of 7ft 6in (2.3m). The code allows underground rooms to be 7ft (2.1m) high. New York law, however, specifies minimum height as 8ft (2.4m) everywhere.

In New York City apartments of three rooms or more, arrangement of rooms is crucial. The building code mandates that there 'shall be access to every living room and bedroom without passing through any bedroom.' Once again, privacy matters, and subjective perception can have as much to do with overcrowding as the actual measurements or layout of a room.

Britain's 1985 Housing Act is the latest chapter in the interesting history of official definitions of small places. When the socially conscious London County Council came under pressure from its finance committee to cut housing construction costs in 1920, they chose to save money by omitting wash basins in bathrooms, by leaving parts of their houses unplastered, and by cutting room sizes to the following:

Living room	144 sq. ft (13.4 sq. m)
Parlour	100 sq. ft (9.3 sq. m)
Scullery	60 sq. ft (5.6 sq. m)
Bedroom 1	144 sq. ft (13.4 sq. m)
Bedroom 2	100 sq. ft (9.3 sq. m)
Bedroom 3	60 sq. ft (5.6 sq. m)

The very existence of a 'parlour' may seem luxurious to the occupant of a small space in a modern city. A tiny city apartment can cost much more than a rural mansion, and the phenomenon is an old one. The London figures above compare unfavourably with the desirable minimum room sizes for a rural labourer's cottage recommended in a 1913 report by the Board of Agriculture. The report's encouragement of 'simple elements of good design which are costly only in thought and care' rather than in cash is one any small-space designer could take to heart.

Tight quarters aren't quite unique to the city, nor are they necessarily the forced result of overcrowding. The tiny dune shack shown below was built in the early 1900s as a quiet outpost on the then desolate seacoast of Cape Cod. Such structures were once inhabited by naturalists, writers, poets, and artists. About 8 feet wide by 10 feet deep, the shack is built on large wooden sill plates and can be dragged along the sand to a better site should the dunes shift dramatically. The drawings reveal truly space-intensive design: plenty of shelves and sheer modesty of lifestyle condense kitchen, bedroom, and office into one room. (From Tiny Houses (Overlook, 1987) courtesy of Lester Walker).

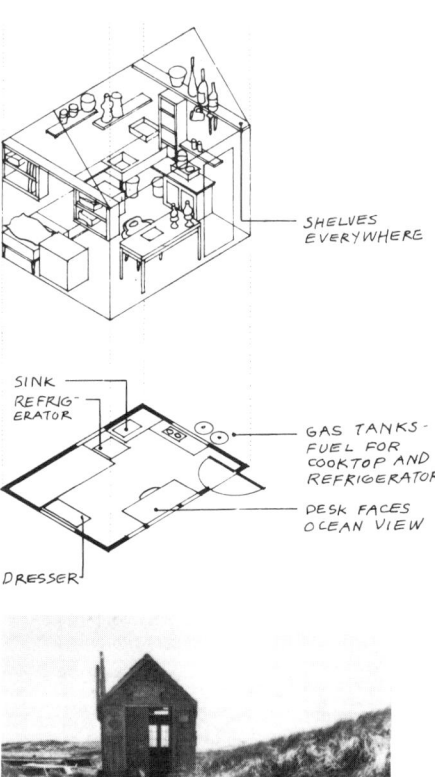

SHELVES EVERYWHERE

SINK
REFRIGERATOR

GAS TANKS-
FUEL FOR
COOKTOP AND
REFRIGERATOR

DESK FACES
OCEAN VIEW

DRESSER

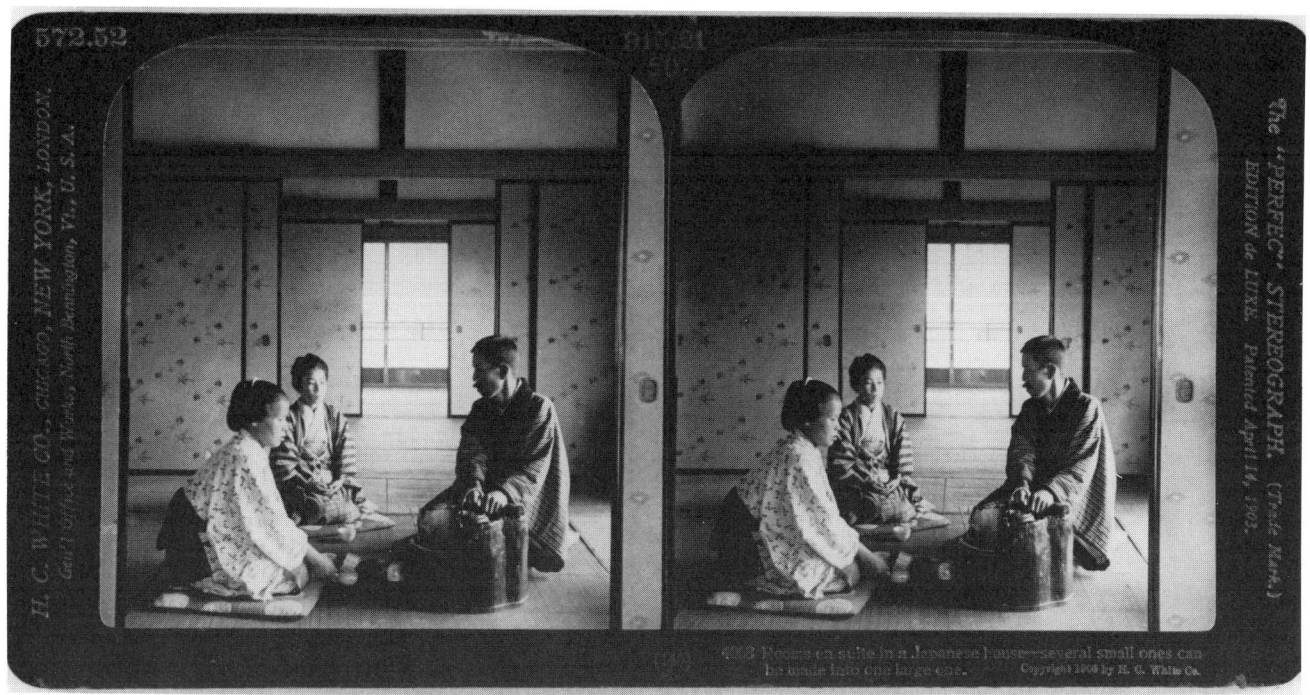

The caption to this 3-D stereo card, made about 1900 when things Japanese were particularly fashionable, reads 'rooms en suite in a Japanese house – several small ones can be made into one large one'. Knowledge of how the Japanese use interior space was to have a great influence on Western design.

The simple, uncluttered, adaptable rooms in the traditional Japanese house are an example to anyone planning a small space. The rooms in a typical nineteenth-century Japanese house, such as the one shown in the photograph (above) are smaller than those in the equivalent Victorian house, but extremely adaptable. The main rooms open into one another, not into corridors, which maximizes use of internal space, and both internal and external walls are considerably less substantial than in western homes. Translucent screens made of lightweight wooden frames covered with paper form the walls. These allow diffused light into the rooms, which can be opened up to the outside by sliding the screens aside in grooves cut into the wooden guiding tracks above and below. The screen is lighter than the standard European or American sliding door, so that it tends to slide smoothly without sticking. Solid, space-eating swinging doors are rare.

The outer screens let in the soft light loved by the Japanese, but they are poor insulators. In bad weather – or at night – wooden shutters could be run in grooves along the outside of the verandah. In winter, thick clothing provided the main means of keeping warm, though a small brazier would be set into the floor. Portable braziers were carried about in boxes and used to keep food warm, to heat water for tea and to light tobacco. The lesson for small-space living seems to be that the portable heating device may be all some people need for cooking. This, however, is an extremely dangerous practice and should never be considered in a cluttered room, particularly if the room is used by the very young, the very old or the very clumsy.

Room size is based on the number of standard 6 x 3ft (1.8 x 0.9m) tatami mats it will take. These substantial mats are about 2in

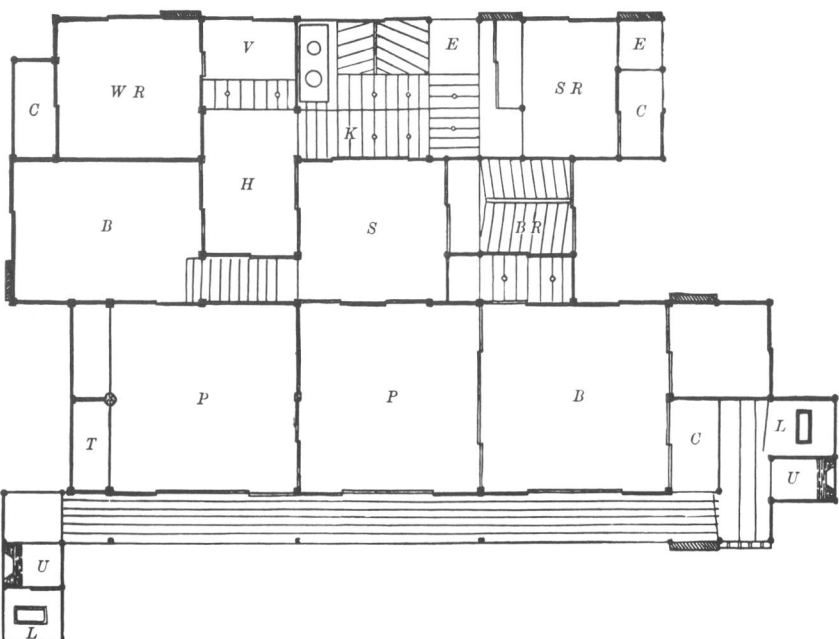

Plan of a house in Tokyo, from Edward S. Morse's classic Japanese Homes and their Surroundings *(1887). The verandah runs across the front of the house, with the main rooms looking on to it. The kitchen and bathroom are indicated by parallel rulings. These rooms have plank floors; all the others have tatami mats.*

(50mm) thick, with a woven straw cover enclosing the stuffing. The Japanese straw stuffing could be replaced by carpet underlay, kapok or foam in a modern western room. The mat will disguise uneven wood floors and provides a quiet, resilient flooring. Mats did not cover the entire house – areas of wood flooring would remain visible.

The Japanese love of apparent simplicity shows in the absence of furniture in the room. At night a futon bed would be rolled out on the tatami mat. The futon (see page 123) has become a popular form of the convertible sofa-bed in the west. Rolled or folded up during the day, it can be used as a seat, leaving valuable floor space free. The Japanese futon would be rolled up in the morning and stored in a fitted cupboard. The sofa has no place in Japanese tradition, where kneeling on the floor makes chairs unnecessary. The only recognizable chairs would resemble western kitchen chairs with the legs sawn and probably with no back.

The habit of kneeling is not easy for westerners to learn, though a low stool with the top sloping slightly forward can ease the problems of pins and needles by keeping weight off the ankles. Any table in the room would also be low and could be put out of sight when not in use.

The absence of furniture makes a small space feel larger and also means the room can quickly be adapted for temporary use for a number of different activities. The fact that all activities take place at low level influences the design of the room. The ceiling can be low (about 6ft/1.8m), and the one or two objects and pictures on display are positioned to be seen from kneeling height, whereas in the west we tend to hang pictures and objects higher on the wall.

Pottery and paintings are displayed in two recesses on one wall – the *tokonoma* (an alcove with a raised floor and lowered lintel) and the *chagai-dana*, a shelf alcove. The objects can be changed according to the season or the guest. This restrained display draws attention to the quality of the few objects on view, and to the floor, the walls, the ceilings and the lighting. The surfaces are natural, and interesting imperfections and asymmetries are sought out. Plaster may be decorative, with coloured sand and clay or chopped hemp fibres added to it to produce different effects.

Objects are designed to be seen in the equivocal soft light passing through the screens. Artificial lighting came traditionally from low-level, mobile lighting, either candles on a stand or oil lamps, with the associated tools stored in the lamp base. There would be no ceiling lights. Low-level lighting is, like so much in the traditional Japanese house, an idea well worth borrowing for your small space.

MAKING A SCREEN

Japanese screens are encouragingly simple to make, requiring few tools or skills. Besides a rule for measuring the space for the screen and the timber to be sawn, only a pencil for marking up the wood, a fine-toothed saw and a chisel are necessary. A metal square to guide the saw will help you saw square joints. This in turn cuts the risk of the screen's twisting.

It is perhaps wise to begin by making a small window screen, which will cut out an ugly view and let in the soft light typical of Japanese interiors. Such a screen can also be used as a cupboard door in front of shelving; a low-wattage light inside the cupboard creates the illusion of a window, psychologically increasing your sense of space.

Larger room-dividing screens are made in the same way, but with layers of paper built up on both sides, the layers being fixed alternately to prevent the frame twisting under load. They sit in wooden tracks above and below. If you have no router to help cut grooves, build up a track using three pieces of timber pinned or glued together. The groove at floor level is only some ⅛in (3mm) deep, that above at least twice as deep to allow you to slot the screen in position. A little wax or candle grease inside the groove will aid smooth running.

The window screen has paper on only one side. The paper could be the traditional 100 per cent pure hand-made mulberry with its long, strong fibres, or a cheaper substitute. Most paper will turn brown quite quickly and is not so translucent. Tracing paper works well but is much more brittle, and screens tend to be prodded by inquisitive fingers and careless elbows.

Choice of wood is important. It must be straight-grained timber, to stop the screen warping. For small screens, strips of hemlock are a good choice. These are sold in various dimensions by modelling shops. For strength, the outer frame should be thick; for elegance, keep the inner framework timber slim, and deeper than it is wide to allow maximum light through without impairing its strength.

All the pieces are joined by halving-joints, in which a notch as wide as the pieces to be joined is sawn out to the halfway point in each piece. The joints in the outer frame are marked and sawn out. Joints in the inner grid are then chiselled out between two sawcuts.

When you have checked that everything fits together tightly, apply white woodworking glue to the joints and assemble.

When the glue is dry, fix the paper. Smear white woodworking adhesive on the wooden strips, roll the paper across and pull it fairly tight. When the glue is dry, spray the paper with water and it will shrink tight. A spray with fire-retardant liquid, available from theatrical suppliers, will reduce the fire risk. The liquid should not discolour the paper.

This traditional sliding window screen in an aggressively modern building by Shin Takamatsu (1984) shows how the paper screen diffuses light coming through the porthole window and blocks out the unappealing view of Kyoto.

The Shaker communities which reached their height in New England and New York in the first half of the nineteenth century lived in simply but beautifully furnished rooms, with much in common with the traditional Japanese interior. The Shakers shared the Japanese delight in the beauty of wood in its natural state; their large windows were often covered with white blinds reminiscent of the Japanese screen, and their use of colour was extremely restrained. Above all, the absence of objects in the rooms makes them feel both calm and spacious. They were hostile to clutter. Everything had its proper place, which is good practice in any small space. They owned few clothes, so the provision of adequate closet space was relatively easy.

The Shakers were in one respect more minimalist even than the Japanese – no decorative objects whatsoever were allowed by the rules guiding the community. Even brass

knobs on drawers were considered too ostentatious.

Shaker craftsmen turned the injunctions against decoration to great advantage, producing some of the most elegant wooden furniture ever produced. The furniture was made in the community's own workshops. They used no veneers, inlays or carving, leaving the wood to speak for itself. The more functional the furniture design, the more perfect it was considered. Comfort was not entirely neglected. A rocking chair was an almost universal feature of the Shaker room, and a comfortable chair deserves its

place in even the smallest space.

Their development of inbuilt cupboards, casters on beds, drop-leaf tables and low-backed chairs which could be stored under the table are all useful examples to today's small-space planner. The Shakers also developed furniture especially for children. The photograph above shows a child's folding bed, a predecessor of the famous Murphy bed (see page 124). While lacking the refinement of the best Shaker furniture – construction is nails and butt joints throughout – this simple piece is a useful design for a small space. In the upright position, held

LIVING SIMPLY: THE SHAKERS

The Shakers' resolute rejection of decoration was an expression of religious belief. The sect, founded in England in 1747, did not develop until it reached America in 1774, where good craftsmanship and elegant design became the basis of their flourishing commercial furniture business. Fake Shaker furniture began to appear by the end of the nineteenth century. The simplicity and calm of Shaker interiors remain the envy of sophisticated designers. The furniture can be imitated or bought as antiques and reproductions but the uncluttered aesthetic is a result of real renunciations. Although they did make innovations (the ball-footed tilting chair and the clothes hanger for example), most Shaker designs are simplifications of existing patterns. It was the way of life the furniture reflected and supported which was the original invention.

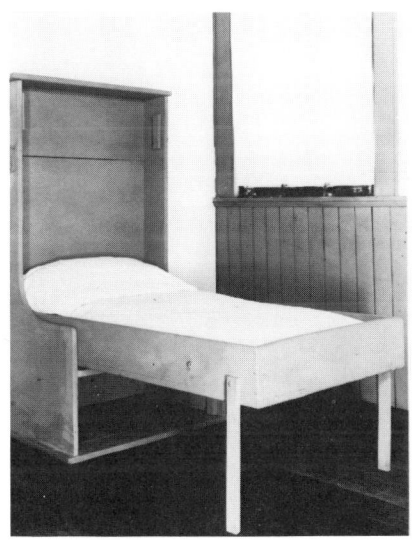

only by the hook (top left) and a matching eye in the bed side, the bed converts instantly into a handsome settle, with storage space underneath.

Perhaps the most interesting Shaker innovation was the pegboard, shown in the two photographs top right. Pegboards lined almost every Shaker room, running around the plain white plastered walls like a picture rail 6ft (1.8m) from the floor. The board is a 3 x 1in (75 x 25mm) pine rail with a small planed beading on the edges. It would be painted 'heavenly blue'. Spacing of the pegs, from which various objects could hang, was variable, but 9in (275mm) was typical.

The elegant lathe-turned, mushroom-shaped maple pegs about 3in (75mm) long are hard for the ill-equipped amateur to reproduce, but door knobs or even dowels are workable alternatives. The range of articles which hung from the rail is quite bewildering: clocks, towel-rails, hats, brooms, mops, tools, and clothes hangers – a Shaker invention which has become an almost universal feature in the western world's closets. For extra space-saving storage capacity the Shakers developed a multi-armed hanger.

The traditional Japanese house gave Western architects a new vocabulary. The floor became a place to sit on, walls became screens, decoration disappeared and reappeared in odd places. New Japanese houses have kept many traditional Japanese characteristics. They have also taken western ideas and reworked them. The unplastered minimalist concrete interiors of Tadao Ando (pages 3 and 24) have relations in the houses of Le Corbusier, who never designed anything quite as punishing as this. The staircase joining the bedroom and living floors is an exterior one. The experience of weather is quite as direct as it was in a traditional garden room, although the spaces you look out onto here are less ingratiating.

Space in modern Tokyo and other Japanese cities is at a premium, and property values there are very high. Even the wealthy are forced to live in extremely small flats.

It is something of a western myth that all Japanese instinctively fold everything neatly away, subscribing happily to a Zen-like ethic of simplicity, requiring fewer possessions than materialist westerners.

Tokyo is in fact a garish and noisy city, full of concrete skyscrapers and not a tatami mat in sight. Most new Japanese interiors have more in common with modern western taste than with traditional Japan. A bulky and unmovable double bed often replaces the futon, and a fully equipped, gadget-strewn, western-style kitchen is common, even though the Japanese still prefer to

House by Akira Komiyama + Atelier R (1983). The stairs join the reception room to a raised study area.

entertain guests in restaurants rather than at home. In traditional houses, glass will often have replaced paper in the lower half of the outer screen wall.

Nevertheless, modern Japanese architects often achieve an interesting fusion of old and new, West and East, and because they frequently have to design very small houses or flats, their work is as relevant to the problems of living in small spaces as their predecessors'.

Architect Koji Yagi designed the flat (right) for a graphic designer who demanded relatively independent domains for himself, his wife, and his daughter, an art student. Her room is as cluttered as any other student room, effectively

countering the myth of Japanese neatness. She has a separate staircase to her bedroom on the upper level. The space under it contains a work space and notice board, with room for a television and radio. The thin radiator under the window saves considerable space.

The hessian chair cover incorporates capacious pockets, an idea which could easily be copied in a home-made loose cover. The exposed steel joist above the door is used for display – as with many successful small interiors, the trick is to exploit tiny areas not normally used.

The staircase up to her father's atelier leads directly into the roof area, opening up a last usable space under the pitched roof. The staircase is a major sculptural detail, rising quickly to the upper floor through the use of oversized steps. The small stairway seems larger by virtue of the sculptural use of light and the exposed steel joists. The roof space is divided into two by glazed doors. One part has a lower ceiling for winter use; the area in the photograph (opposite) has a high gabled ceiling for summer use and serves as an exhibition space.

Architect Akira Komiyama and Atelier R designed the raised and top-lit study area in the photograph (left) at the end of a reception room. It is very small, about 9ft (3m) across and 6ft (2m) deep. On its left is a walk-in closet of about the same size with sliding doors. The circular area behind it is part of a sliding screen which filters the light through from the room beyond, as in traditional Japanese houses.

This room shows a sensitive fusion of old and new. The screen, which serves as both door and wall, gives onto the one traditional room in the house, a six-mat tatami room. The study area, tiny yet eminently practical, is conceived within a schema of minimal horizontal and vertical lines – a reinterpretation of the traditional Japanese aesthetic in modern terms.

Yet another approach is taken by Tadao Ando (pages 3 and 24). His child's bedroom looks terrifyingly austere to Western eyes. Yet Ando has filtered natural lighting through the ceiling, allowing the play of light on minimal space. Although this is a tiny site, 8 x 33ft (2.5 x 10m), he has built a four storey house with shop for a husband, wife and three children. In it he has tried to secure privacy as well as contact with light, wind and rain.

House in Tokyo by Koji Yagi (1983) (below and right).

Minimal living spaces can feel luxurious, particularly if you choose the spartan lifestyle. There is a monastic feel in the nineteenth-century farm labourer's cottage which T.E. Lawrence ('Lawrence of Arabia') rented in 1923 as a retreat. Lawrence lived frugally, partly because of his very real poverty, partly because of his taste for simplicity. The furniture is well made and comfortable, showing that wealth is not necessary for elegance in the minimal style. The photograph (above) shows his esoteric foil-lined bedroom, with its bunk bed on a chest of drawers.

The small, box-like house in Kobe, Japan, built in 1983 by self-taught architect Tadao Ando (left), presents a blank, windowless facade of reinforced concrete to the street, yet the architect thinks contact with natural elements is important. He has said that 'the smaller the site, the greater the need for natural elements. Where there is the matching will to live, a perfect urban life can be created in such a small house.' The surrounding space is certainly important when your house is too small. Even a view can make a great difference. Prisoners committed to the Broadmoor long-term prison are often encouraged by being told there is a nice view from up there! The photograph shows the external staircase and courtyard on the third floor.

A rolling screen of aluminium channel, steel pipe and turquoise-coloured corrugated fibreglass in a New York loft designed by Laurie Hawkinson. The division of large areas into small ones – particularly in deep spaces such as warehouses – can cut out light. This kind of semi-industrial detailing is one solution.

Sliding doors and screens are important space-savers. In the crowded conditions of submarines and railroad sleeping cars, both of which are built – like American railroad apartments – with rooms giving off a long through corridor, there is simply no room for a hinged door to swing. Sliding doors help people move efficiently along the corridors without provoking accidents. It is interesting to note that the luxury compartments for the pampered passengers on the Venice Simplon Orient-Express have hinged doors, whereas the more space-conscious six-berth sleeper cars in the French SNCF trains running on the same route have sliding doors. The sliding door is much safer when there is likely to be someone else on the other side of the door. In the cramped space of a small home, the same safety features apply. The sliding door can prevent accidents.

Despite the high risk of spectacular disasters, food is still routinely moved from restaurant kitchens to the tables through a swinging door, with waiters returning with the debris through the same door. A glass porthole in the door prevents collisions by allowing a laden waiter to see a colleague arriving on the other side. A similar porthole – circular, square or triangular – could be cut into a hollow-cored door at home. Besides improving safety, it lets light into the room and can look good. For similar reasons, the wooden panels in a traditional panel door can be

26

replaced with glass. Safety glass should always be used.

The sliding screen is one of the most inexpensive and effective ways of redefining your small space. Screens will provide instant visual privacy, for example to create a temporary guest-room or to cut off the sight of a kitchen littered with the remains of dinner. Screens and doors that slide and fold are much easier to erect than permanent partition walls; perhaps more importantly, they give you greater flexibility than solid walls, as they can be removed instantly when you want to open up the room to its maximum size.

Fitting a sliding door or screen is not difficult. The instructions given in most do-it-yourself books for fitting sliding closet doors will explain the basic system of grooved channels. These will support a lightweight paper screen. Heavier screens or doors can be hung from a pair of roller brackets running inside an overhead track which is normally screwed to the ceiling or to the walls at each side. A guide track fixed to the floor stops the door or screen from wobbling. Heavier sliding screens and doors, such as glass patio doors, will run in grooves fixed to the floor.

Roller brackets for screen hanging are manufactured for the domestic market, and their self-lubricating nylon wheels should need no oil. However, heavy-duty industrial sliding-door gear can look more striking in a high-tech interior, and it is designed to last. It is essential to hang the screen or door level, to stop it sticking in its track; adjusting

screws on the bracket normally make this a very simple job. Since few floors or ceilings are either horizontal or parallel, these adjustable brackets are a great help.

Glass screens have several advantages over the Japanese paper screen – they let light through, create acoustic privacy, present no fire risk and stop smells – but large sheets of glass can clearly be seriously dangerous. Again, it is essential to use safety glass.

Glass is only one of many alternatives to the rice paper favoured by the Japanese screen-makers. Those daunted by the thought of making a refined Japanese-style screen could save time and effort by using garden trellis as the screen framework.

Room-dividing screens need not slide. The free-standing zig-zag folding screen is a popular alternative. However, it occupies an inordinate amount of space in a small room. The system illustrated in the drawing (right) adds versatility to the classic folding screen. Three or more plain, lightweight hollow-core doors are painted black in imitation of oriental lacquer, and hinged together using lift-off hinges to make the screen. When the owner needs a low coffee table, the end

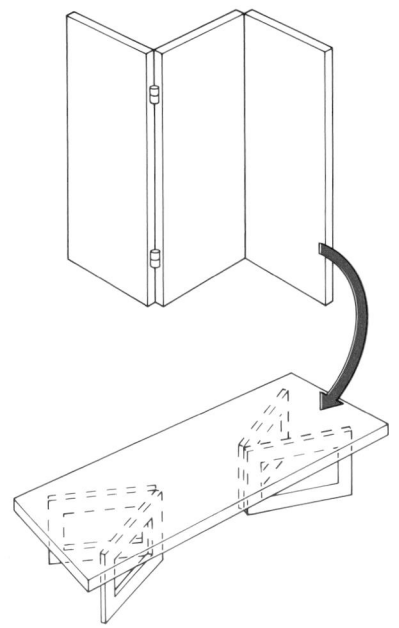

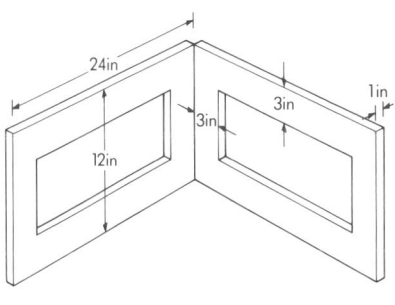

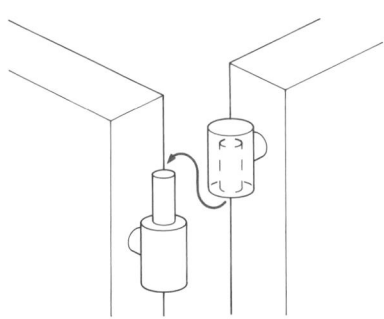

A room-dividing screen can be made very simply by hinging three or more standard hardboard/masonite doors together (top, right). If lift-off hinges (bottom right) are used, a screen panel can be lifted off to become an instant table top (centre right) by placing it on a pair of hinged trestle-type supports, which can be folded away in a closet or hung on the wall.

panel is simply lifted off and placed on the pair of supporting trestles. Each trestle consists of a pair of identical wooden rectangles, hinged together so they fold flat for storage when not in use.

Venetian blinds can be hung from the ceiling and used to divide a room visually. Vertical louver blinds can do the same job when they are drawn across the room to provide a degree of privacy, as in Eva Jiricna's flat illustrated on pages 87-90. Both Venetian blinds and vertical louvers are very unobtrusive when not in use. Both were also designed for window use but they can, just like the Japanese paper screen, be equally effective as internal room dividers. Perhaps the simplest idea to bring into the room from the window is the curtain. If it is long enough, the curtain will also act as an excellent insulator.

Furniture is often a practical way of creating separate volumes within your small space. A set of bookshelves, a worktop counter or even a sofa set across the room can help redefine the space. It may be possible to place tall furniture across the centre of a large bedroom, which would then provide a room for two independent children, while the parents occupy a smaller – but complete – bedroom elsewhere.

Mirrors are a classic tool in the art of illusion and one of the many decorative devices which can be used to make your small space seem larger than it is. Certain architects have exploited the potential of mirrors wonderfully well. Many consider the Soane Museum, built by Sir John Soane in the early nineteenth century

to house himself, his studio and his esoteric collection, contains the finest small spaces in London. The house is littered with lessons for small-space planners. The use of mirrors – in the breakfast room (see opposite) in particular – is only one of many devices for making the interior feel much more spacious than its standard London dimensions would appear to allow. False perspective and changes in axis are other more complex devices deployed by Soane.

The Viennese architect Adolf Loos was another architectural ace of space who used mirrors well. He designed a bar with mirrored walls facing each other, which gave the clients a sense of space and light. However, the mirrors were used only in the upper half of the room, so they were high enough to stop the seated customers being confused or distressed by the sight of endless reflections of themselves when they sat down.

Mirrored walls can be dangerous to those under the influence of drink. Fuddled music fans paying their first visit to the Marquee, the famous and very cramped old rock venue in London's Soho, frequently walked into the mirror wall thinking it was another room. Fortunately there are safe uses of mirrors.

If you place a half-round table in front of a mirrored wall, you not only prevent accidents but you create the illusion of a circular table. Round tables suit small spaces, as they have no sharp corners to bump into. They can also seat more people in the given space than the rectangular table. If you display objects on the table in front of a

mirror, the reflection allows you to see both sides of them at once, an idea frequently exploited by museums, for instance when they are displaying pottery.

The mirror's ability to reflect light can be used to brighten a dark room. Mirrors on the wall opposite the window reflect light back into the room. Mirrors or mirror tiles fitted around the window reveals will fulfil a similar role. Mirrors are also waterproof, and they make bright, easy-to-clean splashbacks in the kitchen, as long as they are protected from heat.

The breakfast room of the house built between 1812 and 1834 by Sir John Soane in Lincoln's Inn Fields, London and now Sir John Soane's Museum. The whole house is a masterpiece of intricate design, and the breakfast room in particular is a sampler of Soane's sleights of hand. (The drawing on page 48 shows it in section). Light comes from a lantern in the centre of the shallow dome which forms the ceiling, although not the whole ceiling, as the room extends beyond the limits of the dome. More light also comes from skylights set above this narrow space. Through a window in this wall you can look through to other parts of Soane's collection (see the urns above the chair on the left of the illustration). The window which seems to be a pair to this is in fact glazed with mirror glass. Strips of mirror run up the sides of the bookcase, and convex mirrors, reflecting the whole room many times in miniature, are set into the dome and line the underside of its shallow supporting arches. All these devices make space ambiguous. It is not so much that the room seems bigger than it is, as that you never quite know how big it is.

If your space doesn't suit your way of living, change the space. Dramatic changes can often be achieved by the removal or addition of interior walls. Removing partition walls is messy but simple, but taking away a wall that is helping to hold the house up – a 'structural' or 'load-bearing' wall – can be expensive and difficult. It requires temporary supports for the ceiling during the demolition, and the installation of a hefty steel girder – an RSJ – across the ceiling to replace the wall. Tenants who take away walls without warning also irritate landlords; to avoid unpleasant scenes, tenants should check with their landlord or the lease before hiring a sledgehammer. (Sledgehammers are, incidentally, too hefty a tool for wall demolition, as they tend to make the whole house shake.)

How can you tell if a wall is structural? There are signs. If you can, climb into the attic above the wall in question. If the wall runs at right angles to the attic joists and is directly under a point where joists are joined together, your wall is a load-bearing wall, and you should proceed with caution. If there is another wall directly above the one you are thinking of removing, there is a good chance the wall is structural. However, if the floorboards in the room above the wall are *not* parallel to your wall, you are probably looking at a non-structural wall.

The problem of identification can be complicated in old buildings, where ground settlement can turn a wall which was originally a simple partition into an important load-bearing wall. If you are in any doubt, call in a building surveyor, engineer or builder.

Possibly the simplest wall to remove is made of wooden studs covered with plaster. Before you attack the wall, make sure you disconnect electricity and water supplies. Hammer off the plaster first, then remove the vertical studs. To do that, take out the nails holding the stud to the top and base plates and wiggle the stud about until it comes free. With the studs removed, the top plate may fall on your head, so leave the two end studs in place until the top plate is out. Finally, take the nails out of the bottom plate and take it away. Do not throw the wood away. It can be used for making a useful piece of furniture for your small space, such as a platform bed.

If the wall is brick, start at the top, and wear goggles and a breathing mask to protect your lungs and eyes. Pay for this safety clothing by selling the bricks you salvage. Nailing together a new timber-frame and plasterboard partition wall is a straightforward job. Look in your how-to book for an explanation of the simple techniques.

Before you build a new wall, bear in mind that the wall will cut light and restrict movement. The positioning of doors and windows is crucial. No new wall should be erected where it will make an existing window look absurd. Consider such unusual alternatives as a wall made of glass blocks. These blocks allow light to pass, but as they are not completely transparent they provide considerable visual privacy. They also have good insulation properties and are easy for the amateur to build. An example of glass blocks in a small flat is shown on page 69.

There is usually enough space inside a partition wall to store shallow items such as audio cassettes or spice jars. There is normally a gap of about 14in (350mm) between the vertical studs in the wall's wooden framework. It is a straightforward do-it-yourself job to open up one side of the wall by removing the plaster or to knock right through to give shelving with access from both sides.

Locate and mark the inside edge of a pair of vertical wooden studs and – having made sure there are no pipes or electrical cable runs inside the wall – mark the top and bottom limits of your wall box and chop out the plaster using a cold chisel or saw. Glue and nail a 1 x 2in (25 x 50mm) batten to the studs at each side, just below the box area. Cut a ¼in (6mm) plywood or hardboard/masonite panel to form the back of the box and glue this in position.

Cut shelves as deep and wide as the opening. Nail the bottom shelf to the battens. the remaining shelves rest on vertical supports glued and nailed to the studs.

A whole series of shelves can be opened up without weakening the structure of the wall. The system can be tidied up by nailing a frame of moulding over the rough plaster edges and studs exposed during the excavation. Alternatively, the box can be covered by a hinged door or a picture, in the wall-safe tradition.

Cornelius Meyer's fantasy of one-room living (see page 4). This is the domestic side of the apartment. Some of the numbered items are: 61, fireplace for smoking meat; 62, hot water cylinder; 63, iron plate to retain heat and to prevent fire; 69, spice and medicine drawers; 72, linen Press; 73, foldaway table; 74, food storage jars; 77, hot and cold water taps; 79 and 80, ovens. The distilling equipment (75) is a piece of the scientific apparatus which figures largely on the engraving of the third wall, which shows globes, scales, a microscope and a telescope.

The organization of life in one room is relatively simple if you live alone – complications come with other people. The way people overcome the lack of privacy, the noise and the overcrowding in traditional single-room dwellings is instructive for anyone forced to share their single room. A lot can be learned from people living on the move, whether they are desert nomads living under the stars or NASA astronauts living among them.

Even mass transportation is as packed with ideas as it is with passengers. The sleeping cars in the movie *Some Like it Hot* prove that it is possible to have a pyjama party in a single berth, but a good night's sleep is normally a higher priority.

The conditions inside the SNCF's (French Railroad) six-berth compartment are the kind which bring about prison reform – six strangers forced to share a space 8ft 5in (2.55m) high, 6ft (1.85m) long and 6ft 2in (1.9m) wide.

(cont. page 35)

The layout of the tiny cabin of a narrow boat is hard to understand in photographs. To make sense of the picture on the right, look at the drawing below. The woman is sitting on the side bed, the table before her is the door of the table cupboard, the pots on the left stand on a stove which rests on the stove shelf, and the curtains behind her can be drawn to divide off the sleeping area. The decorated plates and brightly polished brass were, like the painted rose pattern which can just be made out below the edge of the table on the front of the knife drawer, traditional narrow-boat style, inspired by nineteenth-century rural cottage decoration. The drawing (below) is of a butty – an engineless canal boat. In motor boats the engine occupied a space just in front of the bed space. The accommodation available in working boats was constricted, but when they are converted to pleasure craft the considerable (if narrow) volume of the hold is usually divided up into a string of cabins.

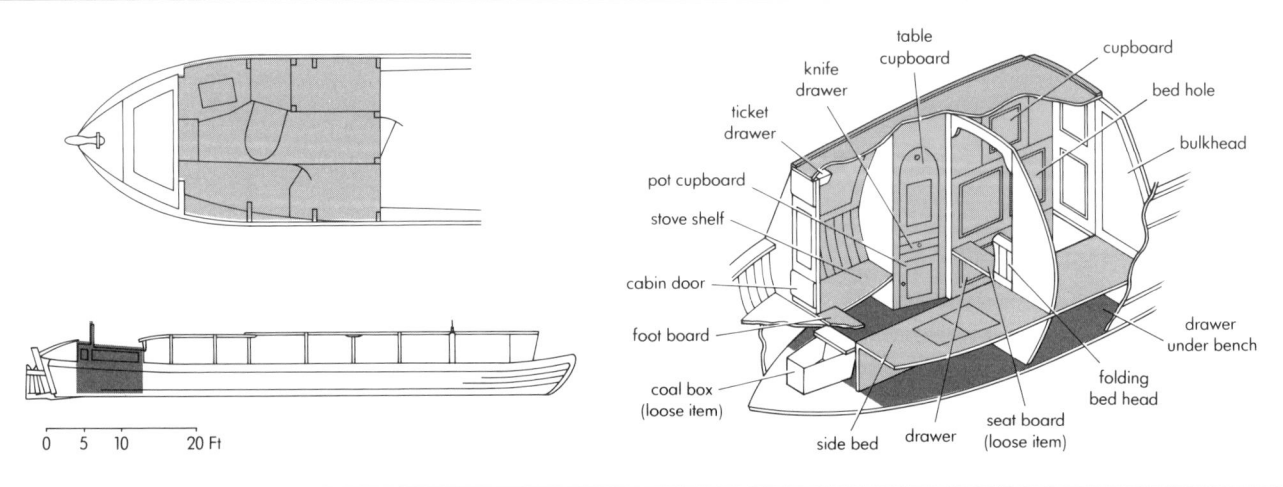

The platform bed in this London apartment (see also overleaf and pages 91-92) has storage below. It is on the right of the door, with the open kitchen on the left. The two form a corridor leading into the room. The storage space above the kitchen unit holds large trunks. The television is on a mobile trolley.

A one-room working and living space for three people in London, showing that you do not have to follow a minimalist, possession-free lifestyle in a small space. The stairs leading up to the bed platform are large, which makes them useful for storage but hard work for the very old or the very young. The top shelf of the book storage system is at picture-rail height, and most of the paintings – which are small – hang above this level. The custom-made, double-glazed French windows keep out noise and let in maximum light; they open onto the roof of the front porch. The stove in the fireplace is the room's only heating. (See also overleaf and pages 91-92.)

The compartment is littered with hidden beds. Beds rise up and drop down on hinges to create two facing tiers of three beds. The support mechanism for the upper beds is ingenious – a flip-out metal block emerges from the wall at each end of the bed. Similar blocks, screwed to the wall, support the bunks in a submarine.

The SNCF design is extremely useful if you want to span a small room – particularly a high-ceilinged room – with a bed which can be removed during the day.

The arrival of the railways led to a decline in business for the canal system in Britain, though slow freight is still carried by the old narrow boats. The narrow boat's tiny cabin is a masterpiece of small-space design, perfected over decades until it reached its present form early in the nineteenth century. As the photograph on page 32 shows, it is traditionally decorated like a nineteenth-century country cottage, reflecting the occupants' poor rural background.

The living accommodation is small, and many admit that life on the narrow boat is tolerable only if you spend most of your waking hours outside, using the country as your living room. The canal banks are also the boat people's traditional supermarket, supplying them with the food which they cooked on the coal-burning stove. The stove also provides the only heating in the cabin, which is small enough to be easy to heat, even though insulation levels are extremely low.

When the food is ready, the bottom-hinged cupboard door, with its circular mirror and country-cottage decoration, flips down to become a table. The table's only support is inside the cupboard, where one end of the table swings up to be stopped under a firmly fixed shelf. The table must be made of solid timber, ideally cut out of the same piece of wood which forms the cupboard front. At home a similar system could provide an ironing board.

There is no bathroom on the narrow boat – the canal and the countryside serve as a communal bathroom, with fresh water supplies available at the lock. Bathrooms, along with fixed supply pipes, drains and sewers, are also luxuries you can't count on in the Sahara desert. A lack of water is largely responsible for people taking to the nomadic life. It is a tragic irony that drought – helped a little by government policy – is now hitting the Saharan nomads hard, threatening life in the age-old tent. Just as the family on the narrow boat uses the outside as part of the home, so the nomad lives less in the tent than in the desert. In a modern city, café and street life grow more lively with over-crowding. Suburban streets stay people-free.

The Tuareg tent of the Sahara is traditionally made of goatskin, but that too is changing. Plastic tents are a common sight in Algeria, and it can be uncomfortably hot inside, since the plastic cannot breathe. There are few furnishings in the tent, as everything has to be carried. The choice of furniture is instructive for small-space livers. For example, there are no chairs; the occupants sit on the floor on rugs or cushions. A few have portable beds, but most sleep on the floor. Loose articles are stored in bags and boxes.

The absence of dominating items of furniture means that the use of areas within the tent is not rigidly defined. There is no 'dining-room' or bedroom, but in many nomadic cultures women and men are allotted their separate side of the tent. Saddles, harness and weapons are kept on the men's side, looms and churns with the women, and no adult male but the husband can cross the divide into the women's side.

In Iran the two sides are divided by a cloth serving as a temporary screen. A division is left in place for a year when a son marries and brings his wife to live in the family tent. After that, they emerge.

A similar division operates in the sophisticated Mongolian yurt, but without any physical divisions. The yurt – or ger – is the dwelling of the great Central Asian Steppe, where it still houses over half the population. Its shape was a strong influence on the development of the geodesic dome.

The typical ger is only 16-20ft (4.8-6m) in diameter, yet it feels extremely spacious, partly because the furniture is low level, partly because of the circular trellis wall about 4ft (1.2m) high, and the sloping roof over which the winter winds slip easily. The dome shape encloses maximum space within a given wall surface area.

Inside there are beds with storage space underneath, cupboards, a low table, stools, washstand and fuel store. The women sit on the right of the entrance door, which faces south west, with the men on the left. The place of honour is the warmest spot, between the fire and the back wall. Lower-status guests sit with new-born arrivals near the draughty door, which suggests that a democratic society should be well insulated!

Insulation in the ger is provided by felt, a Mongolian invention unsurpassed as protection against cold, wind and rain. Being wrapped in felt and fat saved the life of artist Joseph Beuys when his plane was shot down in the Crimea during the Second World War. Beuys also wore one of the great small-space storage waistcoats, covered in pockets and similar to the cobalt-blue suits of flame-retardant cotton worn by the NASA astronauts in the space shuttle.

The organization of space in the shuttle is rather like a high-tech narrow boat floating through space, with a small living area behind a vast cargo bay and below the flight deck. If travel broadens the mind, it certainly doesn't increase the space: all activities are crammed into this single room. Here each crew member must eat, cook, wash, exercise and excrete along with six others.

The shuttle is a good example of defining your problem before you begin looking for solutions. The weightless conditions mean that earthbound solutions such as the three-piece suite are largely irrelevant. It is interesting that the absence of chairs seems to cause the astronauts less distress than having no table, a lesson for the bed-sitting room on earth.

There are beds, but with seven

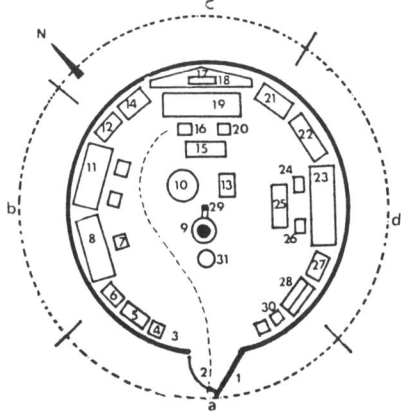

Plan and interior of the one-room, circular yurt – or ger – of the Mongolian nomads. Typically 16–20 ft (4.8–6m) in diameter, the yurt can be erected, according to nomad tradition, in one hour, to provide accommodation for a family, guests and new-born animals. The circular room is well furnished with the essentials of nomadic life, including a display area for sacred images (17 in the plan). The beds (8, 11, 19 and 23) have storage capacity underneath; there are low tables (15 and 25) and stools (16, 20, 24, 26 and 30), cupboards (5, 12, and 14), chests for clothes, bedding and carpets (14, 21, 22, 27), a washstand (28) and a central stove vented trough the dome roof.

crew members and room for only four bunks – or 'sleep stations' – one of them confusingly vertical, astrotech has revived the old naval system of 'hot bunking'; when one person gets up, another goes down.

Even astronauts, despite their famous rationality and imperturbability, need privacy, and they can pull sliding panels or a fabric curtain behind them to shut the rest of the shuttle out of their sleep station. In theory the domestic workload is also shared equally, with cooking duties on a rota system.

Keeping clean and getting rid of waste is important in a small world. Smells can soon build up to high density, and human wastes can be dangerous. The astronaut has a daily change of underwear, a fresh shirt every three days and a personal hygiene kit, similar to those given to prisoners on earth, give or take a deodorant or two. The kit contains a selection of the following:

Shaving Cream – Gillette, Palmolive or Edge Gel;
Razor – Schick Twin Blade, Gillette ouble Edge Safety, Norelco or Remington Electric;
Hair Care – brush, comb, comb-pic;
Skin Emollient – Nivea or Keri Cream;
Stick Emollient – Mitchum, Dial or Ban;
Dental Hygiene – Oral B 40 toothbrush or disposable toothbrush;
Soap – Ivory Bar or non-foaming liquid.

A sunny summer vacation in a caravan can be fun, though the enforced cohabitation and lack of privacy can lead to tensions within

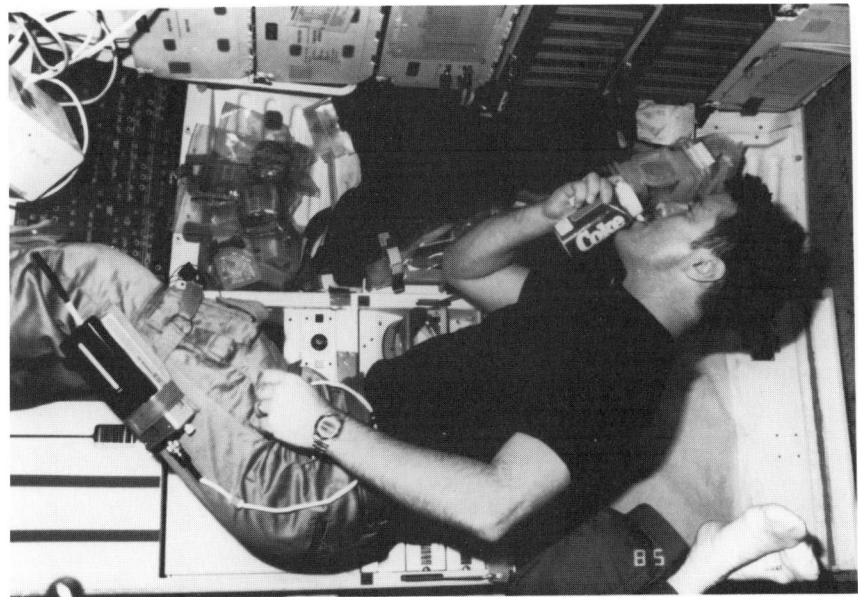

Zero gravity, but high pressure on space: astronaut Anthony W. England tests a carbonated beverage dispenser near the tiny galley aboard the Earth-orbiting space shuttle Challenger (left), and tries to stop a colleague's floating feet spoiling his drink. The living quarters are dramatically overcrowded – a crew of seven sleeps, cooks, eats, cleans and works together in one room. The only privacy is behind the sliding panels of the bunk-like 'sleep stations'.

The NASA reality compares oddly with the padded Victorian comfort of Jules Verne's From the Earth to the Moon *as illustrated in the early edition of the book (below), in which the adventurer travels on his pioneering journey through space accompanied by his dogs, guns, ladder and a tree. One of the few concessions to space saving is the under-seat storage.*

the family in wet weather. However fraught the atmosphere becomes, few caravan tours end in a resurrection of the traditional Romany practice, with mother and children in the beds inside the caravan while the father sleeps under the wagon with the dog.

Fairground and circus operators in the UK travel around the country with their work, and when a caravan is your year-round home, proper organization is imperative. Many of the show people's caravan interiors are extraordinary, showing their skill in decorating an area as well as in putting on a spectacular event.

They are also used to packing things into a tiny space. Within hours of the end of the show the fairground rides are packed up, folded away and on the road again. A 50ft (15.25m) diameter ride can fit on a truck 36ft (11m) long – about the same length as a family caravan.

In such a caravan, the main bedroom would be behind a sliding door at one end – the far end from the entrance door. A small bedroom for the children – perhaps fitted with bunk beds – would be at the other end, an arrangement which brings a degree of privacy to both parties. Between them is the kitchen area and sitting-room, with a convertible bed/settee providing extra emergency sleeping accommodation. Besides the routine television sets, VCRs and telephones, there may be such unlikely details as a full Cotswold stone fireplace, helping to create a traditional English country-home atmosphere in a van where the occupants have never lived in a house. The caravanners will make financial sacrifices to introduce the stone fireplaces, since the vehicle's leaf springs have to be reinforced.

Since the Middle Ages the western solution to the problem of providing the spaces appropriate to the different demands of living indoors has usually been to subdivide: ancient hall houses are divided into rooms, later houses broken up into apartment flats, large rooms partitioned to provide bathrooms, bedrooms, kitchens and living-rooms.

When needs change, subdivision may not solve the new problem. When a person joins the self-employed and needs work space at home, when a baby grows up and needs more room, when the friend who came to stay for a few days never leaves, when you crave a garden, adding on may be the best solution.

Adding on has its own original history, and adding on without devouring land demands the most original approach. The balconies of Hong Kong are perhaps the most striking example of how to borrow space. Block upon block is encrusted with balcony annexes, seizing new space from the air itself as the densely packed population solves its own living needs to provide kitchens, laundries and gardens up and down the façades of high buildings.

This 'barnacle building' is strictly illegal. The idea is comparable to the medieval European approach. In the congested towns where timber-framed houses were tightly packed along narrow streets, overhanging upper floors, tier upon tier, provided more room than the ground plan seemed to permit. Rooms were even slung across the street, linking house to house in a bridge.

More recently, solutions have been as small as the outside meat-safe kitchen extension on a north wall or as large as the lean-to greenhouse which adds a whole new room at ground level, with the balcony and even the window box adding a new dimension to upper-floor living.

The clearest option for extension is often the attic, usually a dusty space in which forgotten objects litter the route to the water tank. The wealthy always saw the potential of these spaces, fitting them with floors and little windows, usually to let in light, not to provide a view. They put rows of beds in the new room to make dormitories for the servants, and called the windows 'dormer' windows. If you live under an attic you have a huge new room waiting to be created.

Before making detailed plans for inhabiting the attic, check on local building codes. Planning permission may be needed, and there are likely to be controls on window size, insulation, floor strength and access — all important points in any case.

The water tank may be occupying the best space, with maximum headroom. It could be relocated. This makes the job less simple but is worth it for the usable space gained.

Loft ladders are cheap and save space, but can be inconvenient. Staircase construction costs more and needs a large landing, but brings the room into the rest of the house. Spiral stairs take least space.

Mansard or gambrel roofs are ideal for attic conversion, with their double pitch, the first stage rising steeply and the second more gently pitched to create a good space for a room. Single-pitched roofs will produce walls which slope in from floor level. Here it may be preferable to reduce the floor area and construct vertical walls some distance in from the eaves. The lost floor space behind the new walls need not be wasted, as it can be used for storage.

Daylight may be more important than view, and skylights are easier and cheaper to fit than dormer windows. If skylights can be fitted front and back you have the makings of a dramatic Gothic lighting effect. Dormer windows, which project out from the roof, can provide sunny niches if the structure is taken down to floor level.

Building on is a more obvious space-creator. In the developing world it is a standard way to build a home, rooms being added as they can be afforded to the basic shell providing 'site and services'. Just as the conservatory expanded thousands of sitting-rooms in the nineteenth century — and also changed the style of the house by providing a new environment — many imaginative glazed constructions are being built in the west today to change and enlarge living spaces, by no means invariably at ground level.

Ready-to-assemble designs in many styles, with wood or aluminium frames, are available from manufacturers for ground-floor or roof conservatories.

Many of these are classified as greenhouses or lean-tos and can therefore bypass the planning laws. Since they need less permanent attachment to the existing building than an additional habitable room,

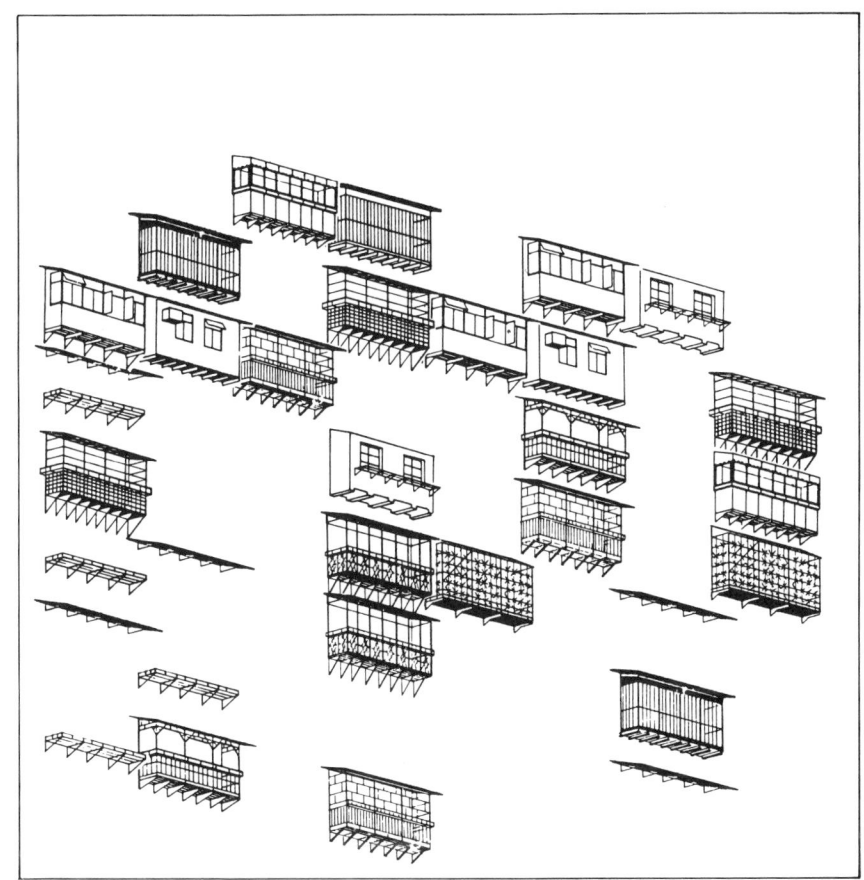

construction can be rapid, inexpensive and relatively simple. They can provide a new living-room, dining-room, playroom or workroom or may simply cover and protect the plants growing on the window sill.

A one-off design from an architect may be much more ambitious. For example, Crowley Moore-Ede changed the quality of a Pimlico, London, house beyond recognition by giving it a sort of glass tent which runs right up the back of the house from a wide sun-room at ground level to the apex where it meets the wall three floors higher. From the front the listed building presents an unchanged nineteenth-century face.

Glass can add a light room without creating an over-dark one inside. There are problems: leaking (look for well-protected joints at every point); condensation (drainage is important); too hot in summer (opening windows, electric ventilation and outside shading can be incorporated); too cold at night or in winter (double glazing will help); safety risks (safety glass).

The cages and balconies projecting from the walls of this Hong Kong tenement building are illegal, and it was decided to demolish an entire quarter of them in 1987. When families commonly live in apartments measuring 325 sq. ft (30 sq. m) the addition of another 40 sq. ft (4 sq. m), at something like a third of the cost of space within the mother building, is a bargain. The cages are fixed to the reinforced concrete frame of the building with expansion bolts, or the frames are welded to the frame of the building itself and grouted. This ad hoc solution depends on a firm basic structure.

This glazed extension to a standard Victorian terrace house in Pimlico, London, gained more than square feet. There is very little space between it and the houses facing, the area was dark and overlooked, and the exhaust of extractor fans from the laundry next door was a problem. The wired glass lets in sun, cuts out air pollution, and allows plants – not bricks – to dominate the view. Extensions like this, which can gain space cheaply because they do not have to meet the insulation and structural requirements of the main structure, can be custom built. It is also possible to use industrial glazing systems, or lean-to greenhouses from the manufacturers' catalogues, which may be both simpler and cheaper. Lighting and heating can be incorporated, and at night greenery can take on some of the functions of curtains. Heat gain and ventilation are important considerations when designing large glazed additions.

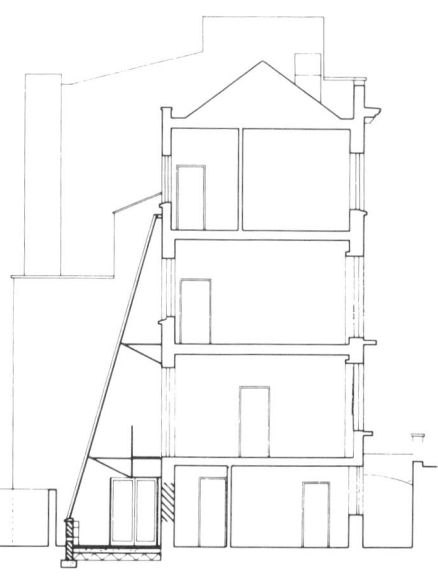

The search for inventive solutions to the problem of fitting furniture to meet all normal human needs into a tiny space can all too easily lead to overplanned and inconvenient solutions. Before filling your room with a battery of miraculously and confusingly convertible furniture, consider whether you really want to push your telescopic desk away into one wall each evening in order to provide enough space for your bed to emerge ingeniously from another.

Clever design can soon merge into overplanning. The illustrations on this and the following page may be over fifty years old, but they should serve as warnings to the over-enthusiastic. The cartoon is by W. Heath Robinson, an early mocker of the Modern Movement, whose book *How to Live in a Flat* still has the power to make designers squirm.

Heath Robinson and co-author K. R. G. Browne define the typical small flat as 'a portion of a house which has been converted but not quite convinced'. Their book also casts a critical eye over new large blocks of flats 'usually resembling Utopian prisons or Armenian glue factories' and looks at the problems of communal living.

The targets of Heath Robinson's attack are dual-purpose furniture and spaces, complex mechanical devices designed to overcome trivial inconveniences, and the sacrifice of human psychological needs and physical comfort to the remorseless logic of space saving in small urban flats.

Heath Robinson's drawings often reflected reality alarmingly closely. The space-conscious small flat in

In 1936, when architectural reductionism had gone to absurd extremes, W. Heath Robinson and K. R. G. Browne published How to Live in a Flat. *This illustration shows an 'economical arrangement of bedroom space in a converted house'. Very human humans inhabit Heath Robinson's gadget-laden cubby holes. They eat at tables let down from the ceiling and get plates out of cupboards built in behind paintings on the wall or keep rabbits and parrots in the space under chairs. A bachelor sits eating on the bottom of his reversible bed and the piano doubles as a dresser. Alarmingly similar ideas can be found in the pages of architectural magazines of the same period.*

The Architectural Review *published the illustrations (below) of Franz Singer's two-room Viennese flat in 1935. The lower illustration shows the work area with folding table, armchair ready for action and desk lamp in position. The upper illustration shows them packed away, with the sliding door to the next room open. The Dilemma on the right, which is, in the words of the manufacturers, 'something more than a practical six-hook clothes stand, because it becomes a helpful stepladder' is a modern version of this kind of thinking. Heath Robinson would have recognized both.*

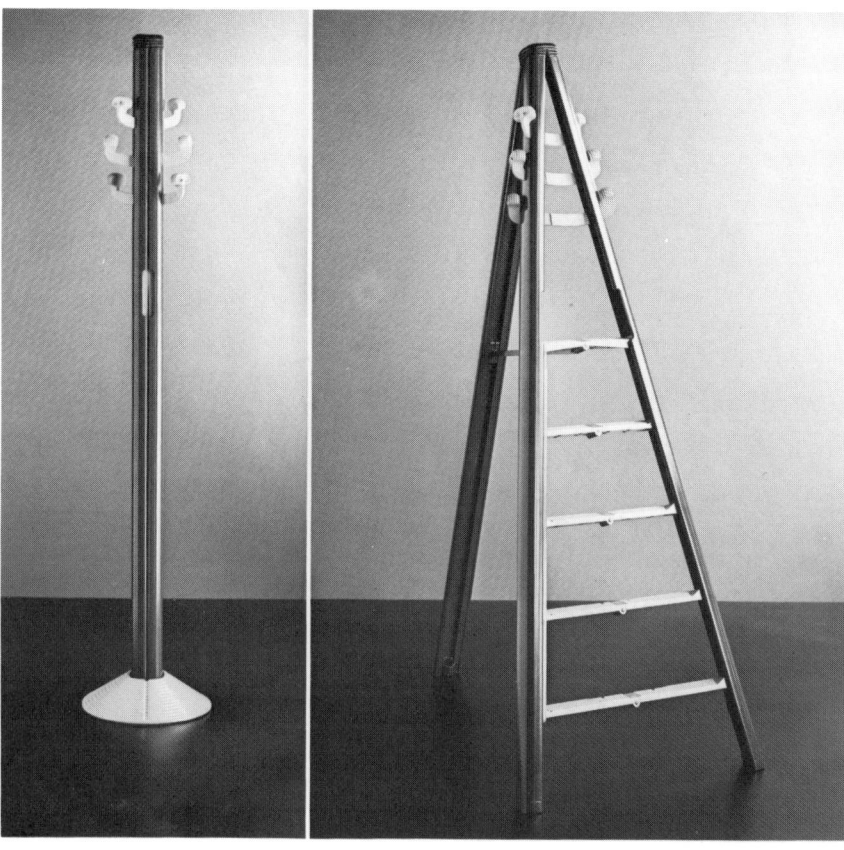

Vienna built in the early 1930s (see photographs on this page) looks in some respects like a three-dimensional Heath Robinson drawing. The writing desk emerges concertina-like from under the bookcase, and the back of the chair flips up for service. Although such a design undoubtedly imposes tidy living on the occupant, and certainly bears witness to the ingenuity of its designer, many might feel that it also makes the human being condemned to live in the room undesirably active in a space meant for relaxation.

Examples of the attitudes Heath Robinson ridiculed are uncomfortably common today, with fresh examples routinely on view in the world's furniture exhibitions. At the 1985 Milan furniture fair critics admired a hatstand which converted into a stepladder. Few asked why. Perhaps the last word of warning should go to American comedienne Abby Stein: 'I was after a convertible sofa-bed. I got a convertible water-bed. It's great. It folds up into a toilet.' Heath Robinson would have understood her delight in the discovery.

Whether you are moving into a new home or considering altering the small space you already call home, the first step is to inspect the building. The information gathered in your inspection can help you plan the most cost-effective changes to your small space. Faults discovered need not be depressing – a roof which has decayed beyond repair, for example, is an opportunity to redesign the attic space, creating an extra room. If the electric wiring is too old to be safe, you are free to rethink the whole system.

Experts can be employed to survey the scene, but the paid expert can never bring to your problems the same selfish passion which inspires your own judgement. You can, with a little care and preparation, carry out a perfectly adequate inspection of your building, both inside and out. Studying the house will stand you in good stead when you plan alterations and improvements.

The only truly thorough survey is complete demolition, well beyond the practical limits to how far you can tear the place apart looking for trouble. Fortunately, a few basic tools will help you uncover most of the information you need. No hard hat or theodolite is required; the only useful hardware will be a checklist of the points you want to investigate, a pair of binoculars to examine the roof from the safety of the ground, a penknife or old screwdriver to probe rotting wood, and a flashlight to help you look into gloomy corners.

Try to carry out your inspection on a rainy day when the full splendour of leaking gutters, pipes, window frames and roofs will be on display. Begin on the outside and be systematic.

ROOF

A look at your neighbours' roofs can be illuminating. If they are all new, the chances are that your own roof will soon need similar treatment. Roof problems must be dealt with quickly before roof timbers rot and ceilings stain and collapse. Repairs to old roofs can prolong their life, but they are notoriously short-lived, and the roof may sustain fresh damage during repair. Consider alternatives – renewal, or making a new room in the attic.

Scan the roof carefully using the binoculars, checking for spots where rain could penetrate. Look for: cracked, missing, slipped, falling or broken slates or tiles; dislodged ridge tiles on the roof apex; sagging roof apex; slipped hip tiles; damaged flashing where the chimney meets the roof.

Lead or copper clips holding the base of slates or tiles show that the slate or tile has fallen off and been replaced, which could be an early warning of a general failure in the nails holding the slates to the roofing timbers.

The timber around the roof could have decayed. Look for signs of rot on the fascia board under the eaves.

CHIMNEY

Years of exposure to driving rain, frost and hot smoke can leave a chimney-stack weak. Careless television aerial installers may have aggravated the problem. The binoculars should reveal cracks in stacks and chimney-pots. In high winds loose pots pose a serious threat to passers-by.

Rain forces its damp way in at the junction of stack and roof, leading to stains on the chimney-breast indoors. Leaning chimney-stacks should be rebuilt or, if the fireplaces below are no longer needed, removed. Pots above unused chimneys should be covered to keep rain and inquisitive birds out of the flue, and the chimney-breast should be ventilated with an airbrick.

GUTTERS

Gutters are hard to reach and easy to ignore. They should slope gently towards a downpipe and be firmly fixed to a fascia board with brackets at least every 3ft (1m). A dripping or overflowing gutter can soon bring trouble by the bucketful when leaves and other rubbish clog them up. The wall below a dripping gutter will soon be soaked. Damp will penetrate the wall, damaging interior decorations and, more seriously, seeping into the timber joists inside the building, leaving them weak.

In dry weather, stains or moss patches on the outside wall will betray bad gutters. Stains at the joints of plastic gutters normally mean leaks. Heavy old cast-iron gutters rust and fail in time. They can be replaced with lightweight plastic.

Cleaning out guttering is simple, but debris should not be swept into the downpipes.

DRAINAGE

Wall-mounted drainpipes must be secure. Cracked or rusty pipes need replacement. Check them closely for corrosion, particularly at the back where painting is easily neglected. A prod with the screwdriver should pierce faulty pipes.

At ground level, note the positions of manholes and drainage runs. These will influence the repositioning of bathrooms and kitchens. Make sure water from pipes discharging into open drains flows away fast. A plumber can carry out a cheap drains test on the underground section of the system, where problems can grow unseen for years. You can learn a lot by lifting up the manhole cover and looking inside. This is the point where drains meet and change direction; it should be clean and sound, with absolutely no cracks showing in the brickwork and no loose concrete.

Ask a friend inside the house to flush the wc – water should neither dawdle nor race through the manhole.

WALLS

Bricks and mortar are porous materials which absorb moisture when it rains and release it to the air as they dry. The lime mortars in the walls of older houses could be very weak and loose. Damage is most likely under the eaves, beneath windows and at ground level. It will show as loose mortar and damaged bricks. Crumbling mortar should be raked out and the wall repointed, a straightforward job but one which takes a long time and can be extremely boring.

If the water in sodden bricks freezes in the winter, it will expand and splinter the brick. Crumbling

bricks provide an easy route for water and should be replaced.

Water penetration will be visible on internal decorations, unless these have been recently renewed, so beware of new wallpaper.

WINDOWS

Rattling and rotten windows let in damp, draughts and noise. Wooden window sills and frames can be tested for decay by probing with the screwdriver. Defective putty – easy to replace – can lead to water penetration and rot, but wet rot is much less serious than its dry relation. Cracks in the corner of window panes often indicate that the house is on the move.

It is easy to replace panes or broken sash cords, but sagging under the window can be costly to repair and could justify complete replacement, which may give you the chance to increase the size of the windows. Enlarging windows can increase light levels inside, even giving access to a walk-in conservatory. Window sizes and styles are covered by local building codes. Check codes before you make an expensive mistake.

INSIDE INSPECTION

The first thing to examine inside, if you have the opportunity, is the present occupant. Ask about recent repairs and improvements, with particular reference to the plumbing, electrical wiring, roof and damp/woodworm treatments. Old wiring will almost certainly have to be replaced. If you plan radical alterations buying someone else's new wiring is of little use.

WALLS

Time and damp crack plaster and stain paper. Bear in mind that pre-sale decoration could simply hide faults. Where fireplaces have been blocked up, check for damp patches. Check the thickness of the walls, and establish the method of wall construction. Hollow partition walls are easier to remove than solid ones, though they may be structural. If you suspect that structurally vital walls have been demolished, take professional advice.

Stains over the baseboard are likely to be caused by rising damp. Prod baseboards, checking for the horizontal crazing which means dry rot is taking it over. Sniff inside the still air of cupboards for the characteristic musty smell of dry rot.

Small cracks in wall plaster are insignificant and not too hard to hide. Tap around any cracked or bulging plaster. If the noise is hollow, there's more work to be done. On a small scale this is easy.

WINDOWS

Windows warp, rot and stick. Open all the windows in your home to see if they work smoothly without being loose in their frames. Warped frames are extremely hard to straighten.

ATTIC

Look up at the roof without using the flashlight – any gaps will show up as points of light. Tread carefully, for rain may have weakened the timbers. During a heavy shower, drips will pinpoint leaks. Use the light to check the rafters, floor and walls for damp. Look out for tell-tale powdery trickles and flight holes in timbers, which are the work of insects – easy to treat in the early stages. Search for birds' nests, remove them, and block up the birds' entrance.

Look at the water tank. The older galvanized tanks corrode with age. Old lead plumbing systems will have to be ripped out. A rotten system could encourage you to rethink the position of the kitchen and bathroom it supplies.

DOORS

Doors should be straight and fit neatly in their frames. Warps are hard to rectify. A twisted door frame may be the result of settlement. The entrance door may have warped or rotted in the sun and rain. It is worth restoring, as visitors take a long look at it while waiting for you to answer the door.

FLOORS

Do not be blinded by the quality of the floor coverings. It is what they obscure that matters. It is often impractical to lift carpets and floorboards, but there are still certain things you can discover. The first thing to establish is what the floors are made of – usually concrete or floorboards nailed to wood joists. Concrete gives you less flexibility for rerunning pipework and electrical cables. Look for signs of rot and woodworm in wood floors. A bouncy wooden floor may be unstable, but most creaks are easy to silence with a few nails.

STAIRS

As on the floor, creaks are more irritating than alarming, but a

rickety staircase sloping away from the wall with a trembling handrail could be dangerous. Traditional staircases occupy a huge amount of space; consider alternative methods of access to upper floors before renewing an aged staircase.

PLUMBING

If an old system or outmoded fittings require replacement, you may want to move the kitchen or bathroom. Check that stopcocks are working to turn water off in case of disaster. Open the cold water tap in the kitchen and bathroom, and turn the supply off where the water enters the house – if the water flow dries up immediately, the taps are supplied directly off the main; if they continue to run for a while, they are supplied from the cold water tank.

Try all taps and fittings for hammering and other strange sound effects which could drive you insane.

Check the fittings, looking specifically for cracks in the bath and its enamel. A tap left dripping for years will damage enamel, and re-enamelling is rarely successful. Check for cracks in the basin and WC, often betrayed by damp around the WC base. Drop a few pieces of paper into the pan and check its flushing power. Examine caulking around baths, basins and sinks, where water may soak through. Find out how the water is heated.

HEATING

How is the space heated? Redesigning the system may make the space more convenient as well as more comfortable. Plug-in electric fires and oil heaters may be useful

mobile stand-bys, but an inbuilt system is preferable, and it will need proper controls – thermostats and timers – to give full value and comfort.

Neglected boilers over ten years old are unlikely to last much longer. Radiators and pipes of a similar vintage may be blocked with scale in hard water areas. Look for rust around radiator valves. Radiator positions can be changed without much disruption.

Neglected fireplaces can be modernized or repaired. Old fireplaces should be approached with caution, particularly in small spaces, where fuel storage can be a bulky problem. Removal of the chimney breast can liberate a lot of space. Missing front bars and cracks in the basket are more inconvenient than dangerous, but burned-out side panels and a broken fireback can lead to hot spots and a conflagration when you light the fire. Firebacks can normally be replaced by lifting out the basket and dropping in a new brick – if you can find one of the right size. For safety reasons, the flue should be cleaned and checked before a fire is started.

ELECTRICITY

Note the position and number of electrical socket outlets – including a special circuit for the cooker – lights and light switches. In an old house they are unlikely to be adequate for today's demands. It is often easier to rewire entirely than to upgrade an ancient system. Do not be tempted to overload sockets. If the lighting is old and gloomy, it should be changed.

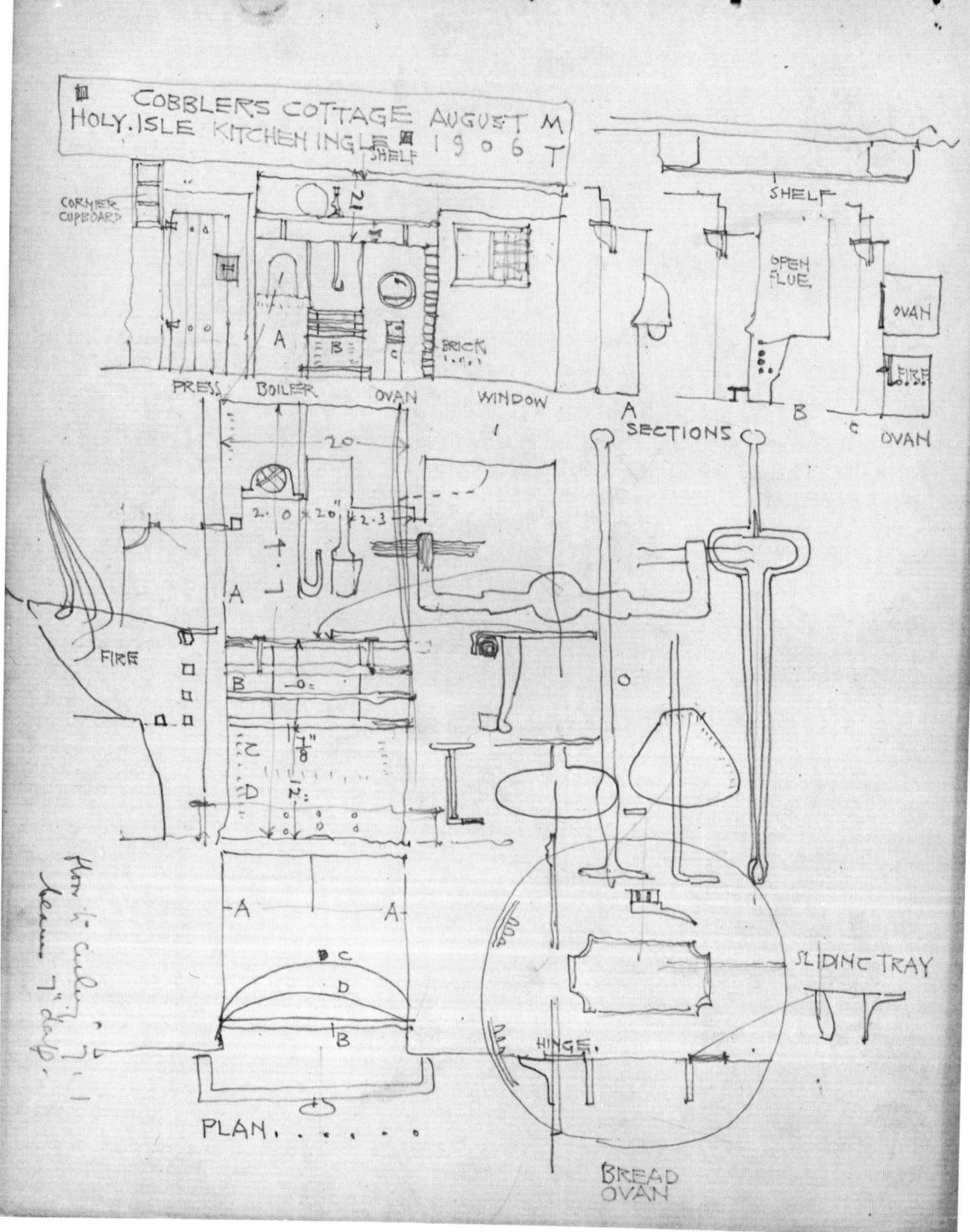

COBBLERS COTTAGE AUGUST M
HOLY. ISLE KITCHEN INGLE 1906 T

CORNER
CUPBOARD

SHELF

SHELF

OPEN
FLUE

OVAN

FIRE

A

B

C

PRESS   BOILER   OVAN   WINDOW   A SECTIONS   B   C OVAN

BRICK

FIRE

PLAN . . . . . .

HINGE

SLIDING TRAY

BREAD
OVAN

Charles Rennie Mackintosh made this drawing (left) of a cobbler's cottage on Holy Island in 1906. It is a masterpiece of architectural draughtsmanship which records a great deal of information with great economy. The top part of the drawing is an elevation of the end of the cottage, with, to the right, three sections through the fireplace, showing how the oven, flue and boiler are built in. The section directly below the elevation gives dimensions and a general plan of that end of the cottage. The rest of the page is given over to larger-scale details of the grate. This kind of sketch is a very good way of looking at details you wish to borrow from an existing building.

The plan below is of an early version of the bathroom illustrated on page 106. Manfred Wolff-Plottegg's drawing matches the precision of the tilework. These very different drawings – one recording an existing building and the other specifying a new one – show how the style of drawing can be adjusted to suit its purpose.

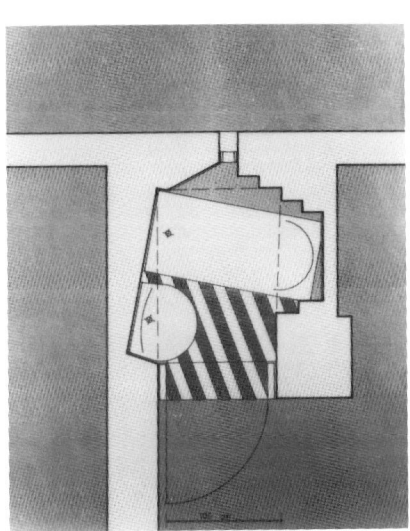

Architects and designers use drawings – sketches, plans, sections, elevations, axonometrics, isometrics, perspectives – as well as models and photographs, to see what spaces will look like, to work out sizes and shapes, to calculate costs, to instruct builders, and to show planners and clients their thoughts. As your own designer and client you should too.

First draw the space as it is. Then use these drawings as the basis for drawings which show how you want to change it.

DRAWING WHAT IS THERE

The most useful drawings are those you understand, even if they are embarrassingly bad. One way of surveying the space you are planning to convert is described here: if you follow these instructions you will have produced enough information for a builder, electrician, plumber or joiner to understand in general what you are after. The plan will not give the fine details of construction, but it will show how the space is to be arranged. If special joinery or major structural alterations are planned, you may want the builder or cabinet maker to submit working drawings.

MATERIALS

A measuring tape or folding rule. If you are measuring on your own, a folding rule is easier to handle. When you are measuring a number of points along a line (window, door and fireplace openings on a wall, for example), running measurements are often more accurate, and for these you need a tape as long as the wall being measured.

A foot rule (for use with folding rule in measuring profiles).

A length of cord for measuring diagonals and small interior dimensions.

A builder's level.

Paper. An A4 pad of tracing-paper or detail paper (detail paper is not as transparent as tracing paper, but is thin enough for a printed scale grid to show through). Either will take a fair amount of rubbing out. An A4 page (working on a scale of 1:30) is big enough for a plan of a room 27 x 17ft (8.2 x 5.2m).

Graph paper to a suitable ruling will enable you to draw rectangles without the help of T-square and set square. Hold the tracing-paper to your graph paper with pins or masking tape to stop movement.

Pencils and felt tip pens. Draw in pencil first – you can rub it out. Coloured pens are useful to key in services, and to colour areas which you want to emphasize.

Some standard architectural symbols may be useful, to show windows and doors, for example. You can borrow books which show these.

SURVEYING THE SPACE

Measuring and drawing. You can begin by making a rough sketch, then add dimensions to this and finally do your neat version.

1. The plan. Starting from the corner to the left of the entrance door measure all four walls. Measure maximum dimensions. Do not stop short at the skirting board/ baseboard, and measure into bays. Draw this rectangle to scale on your pad. If there is any doubt about the room being square, measure the

diagonals. If these are not equal the room is not rectangular. You can draw its true shape by seeing where wall and diagonal cross.

Now measure the openings and projections: bays, chimney breast, doors and windows.

The scale we are working on is large enough for the mouldings round doors to be shown, and skirting boards/baseboards can be indicated. If you are planning furniture to stand against a wall the thickness of the skirting/baseboard can be significant – it can reduce the width of a bay at floor level by an inch or so.

Show how the doors swing, and if there are casement windows show on which side they are hinged. Draw in radiators and any other non-movable hardware, and show any significant changes in the floor – of level, for instance, or if it changes from tile to wood at any point.

Show the thickness of the walls. This is not always easy to work out, as you will usually have to measure the thickness of a wall at an opening, and then deduct the thickness of the mouldings which surround it.

Make a plan of each room (or passage), always incorporating a bit of one drawing (usually a door and party wall) in the next one.

If you need (or want) a plan of the whole space, when it comprises more

Plan and section of the Soane breakfast room. The photograph on page 29 shows the part of the room represented by the left-hand side of this plan. What is not clear in the photograph is the fact that there are skylights above the spaces to left and right of the dome. This combination of plan and section is one of the best ways of describing a room on paper. You can include elevations for all four walls if you wish, each projecting from its own side, like folded-down flaps. In this drawing the design for the plasterwork in the ceiling is shown in the plan.

The plates in Jan Vredeman de Vries's Perspective *(right) include the construction lines. The view is that of a standing person whose eyeline (the horizon – 'Orison' in the illustration) thus coincides with the eye-height of the standing figures.*

than one room, it can be made by tracing the survey drawings of each room in their correct relative positions.

2. The elevations. (The elevations are to the walls what the plan is to the floor). You already have the position of openings, bays and so on drawn on the room plans. Take the plan (turning it if necessary) and draw the line which indicates where floor joins wall. Measure the height of the room and draw lines up at each corner to the ceiling. Complete the rectangle. If there is a cove moulding where ceiling joins wall, show how deep this is.

Now draw in the vertical lines which indicate the corners of bays, and the sides of doors and windows. Complete these rectangles too, to the same degree of detail: show mouldings, skirtings, and sills.

There is usually no need to draw a ceiling plan, but you can plot the position of the ceiling rose, if there is one, on the floor plan.

Sections, which are like elevations but show a cut through a room at a given line, give information about floor thicknesses (most easily measured in the stairwell) and wall thicknesses. One drawing can combine elevation and section.

As the drawing is to scale, distances you measure on it will give you the real distances in the room. It is a good idea to include notes of measurements on your drawing, both as a check against inaccuracy and to give information about details which are too small to be read easily from the plan itself.

3. Tracings. These survey drawings are the basis for drawings you will make to show what is to be done to the space. Architects make tracings to transfer the information on one drawing to another. It is sometimes better to have two clear drawings *(cont. page 53)*

The axonometric drawing on the right shows the New York apartment which is illustrated in the colour pages following. (There is more about it on page 85). Stereographic projections like this one combine information from plan and elevation. In a perspective drawing parallel lines converge. Here they do not, so vertical heights and horizontal distances are all to scale. The bottom section of the drawing shows the whole apartment, with the front wall pulled forward. The top section shows the two floor levels separately. Axonometric drawings like this are good at showing how parts fit together and are easier to construct than true perspectives.

The colour illustration (opposite) shows the view into the street from the front of the apartment (on the left in the drawings). A simple two-stage staircase was constructed to give access to the apartment's upper level without cutting out the light through the street windows. The platform designed by architects Henry Smith-Miller and Laurie Hawkinson is suspended from the cinder block ceiling by aluminium poles, an interesting alternative to the standard floor-mounted structure. The bolts supporting the platform are visible on the second colour photograph (overleaf), which also shows the two sets of sliding, floor-to-ceiling Japanese-style shoji screens which allow the spaces to be changed instantly. Each set of four screens can be used in four positions. By sliding the screens in their aluminium channels, the library can be linked to the bedroom or the dining area.

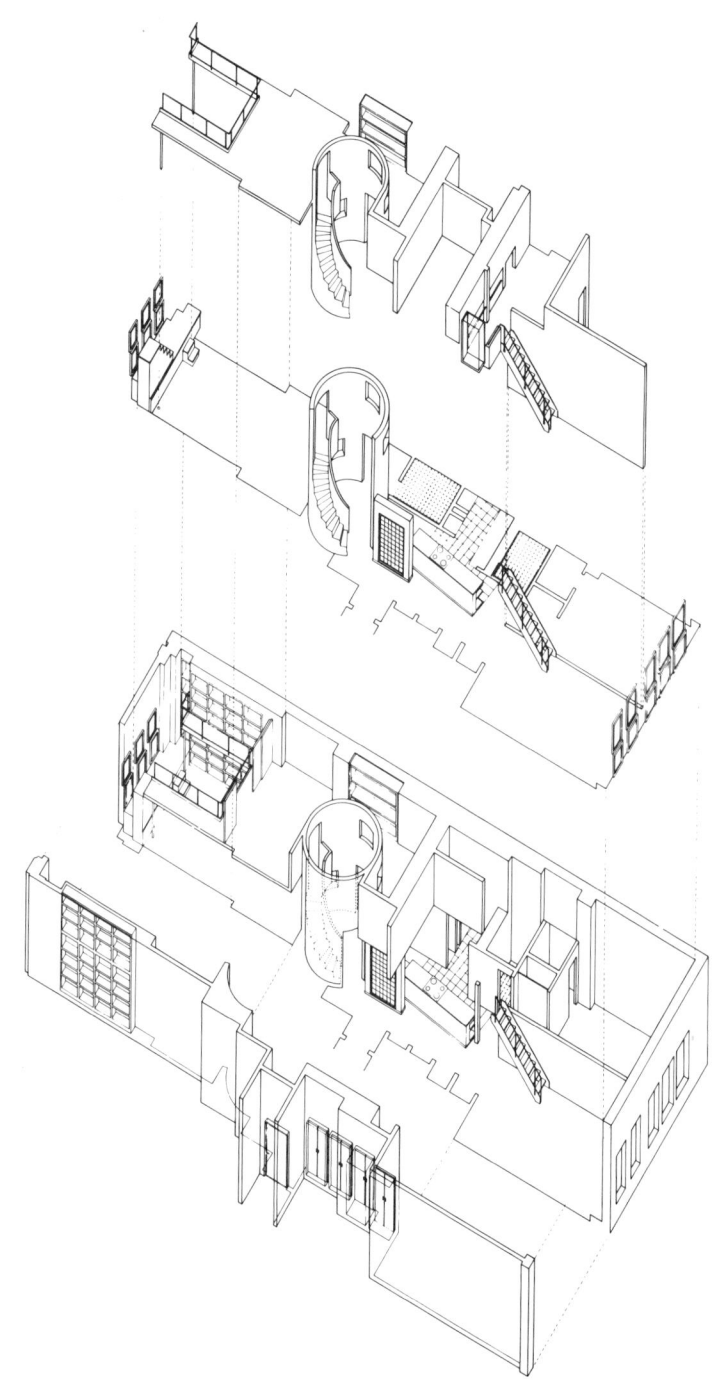

than one cluttered one, but simplicity has its dangers, and plumbing and wiring, for example, set out on separate drawings, could be found to be dangerously entangled when the final work was done.

Simple perspective drawings, like photographs, might seem more understandable, and they can be the only way of conveying any meaningful idea of a space with curving walls such as the narrow boat cabin. The main problem is that they are harder to do.

Annotated photographs have proved to be extremely cost-effective in rehabilitation projects in the USA, as they avoid hours spent drawing details of complex mouldings and fittings which must be matched. They will probably be a useful addition to your drawings.

Simple models made of card offer in many respects the ideal solution. Some of the century's most prestigious architects have used models to see what their ideas would look like in three dimensions. Mies van der Rohe hung a glass model of a building outside his office window to see how the reflections would work, and he built a full-size on-site model in canvas and wood of his design for a house in Holland. It was rejected, which saved the client a lot of heartache and money.

To make a model, draw your plan and elevations on card, cut them out and fit them together in three dimensions. You can move model furniture around inside, remove walls and construct new partitions. It is a lot easier and cheaper to reject ideas than to rebuild walls.

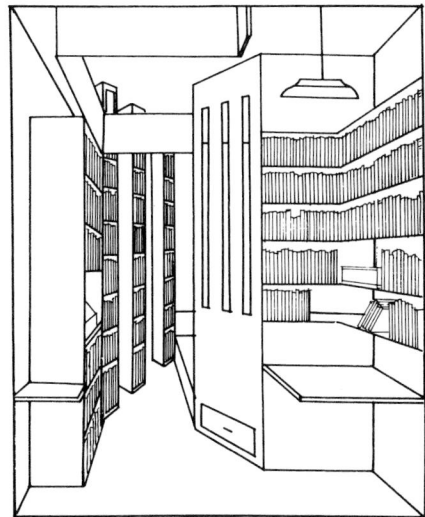

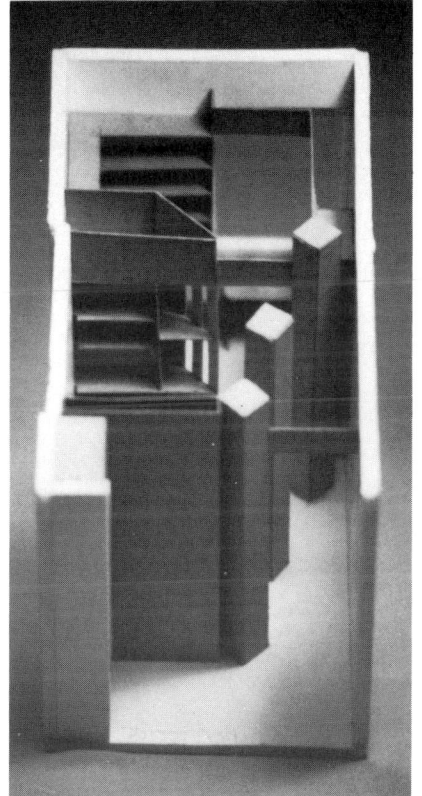

Next, survey yourself and your lifestyle. If you are making things for yourself, you can get them right. Standard furniture – which may not fit into your small space – tends to be a compromise posing as normality.

Work has been done on the minimum space needed for certain activities, such as getting out of the bath and making the bed, useful information even if you do not want to do things in the standard way. There are manuals devoted to these figures. You need not take them too seriously. The main lesson is to be aware of how you do things before you build.

Your own likes and dislikes will certainly affect your design. Do you need a vast kitchen with space for glamorous dinner parties? If you stay out all the time eating hamburgers, a small kitchen will do. Do you want room for friends to stay? When you have decided what activities are going to take place in the space, you can decide where to fit them in.

Some of your space may be

The perspective drawing (above) shows an adventurous solution by New York architects Cobuild to a Manhattan writer's problems – working without being tempted by the sight of the bed, sleeping without being faced by his work, and feeding his dog, all in one room. The columns hold books and break up the view. The simple cardboard model of the room (left) was given to the client so he could decide for or against the columns. After looking through the model with and without the columns, he bought them. Such models are easy to make, need no decoration and can help you pinpoint problems in a proposed design.

underused. To check this, you could mark a week's movements on tracing-paper laid over the plans, with a line showing every movement from place to place and a blob marking points where you stop. Where there are concentrations of blobs, you may need more space. Look for unmarked areas; these are the ones your reorganization could exploit. Test various layouts with this system until you find one where the pattern is even.

Now you can decide on methods of construction, what you can afford, how long it will last if you do it in a certain way and how much maintenance it will require.

The first move if you have just started living in a new and empty space is to get to know it, whether you have just been allotted your own room in your parents' place, moved into your first apartment or moved out of the big old family house into a small retirement home. Take your time. Get some sense of what it is like to sit in various parts of it. Work out where it is noisy, draughty, dark and sunny.

Savannah, Georgia, is one of many historically interesting towns throughout the US and Europe engaged in the restoration of their old buildings. Budgets are often as limited for the major civic restoration project as for the individual's home-improvement plan. To cut costs – and save time – without lowering quality, the Savannah Landmark Project followed the example of other similar schemes and used annotated photographs (right) of the buildings in the Victorian district, rather than measured drawings, to instruct the builders.

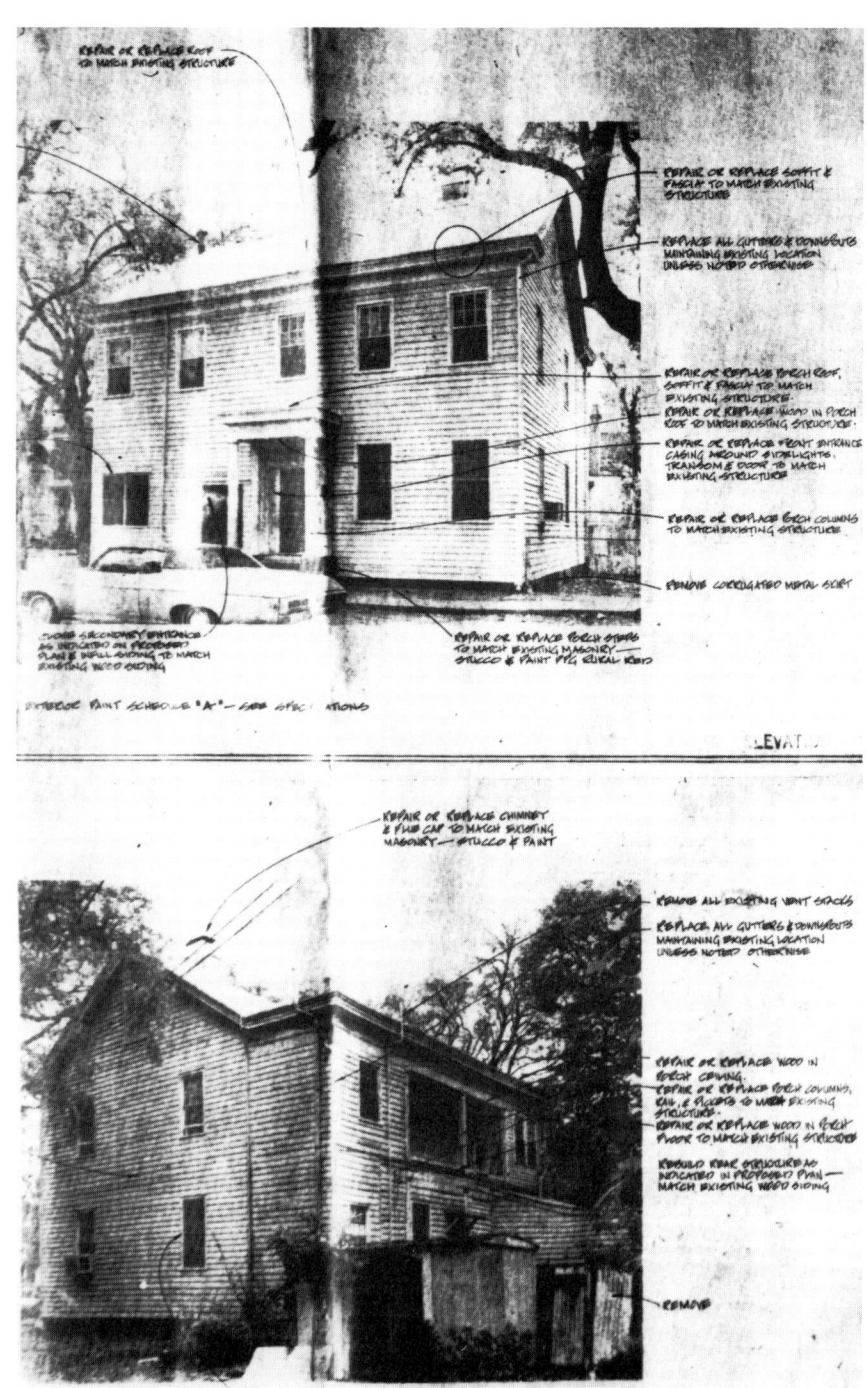

Houses at various stages of completion on the south London site, 1986 (above). Each self-builder works at his or her own pace. Note the absence of cement mixers and heavy machinery. The houses are built with basic tools and basic skills.

The thought of planning and building a complete house, however small, in your spare time would terrify most normal people. The fears of even the utterly inexperienced amateur could be calmed by a look into the simplified self-build system developed over the past twenty-five years by British architect Walter Segal and his partner Jon Broome. Their system has enabled many unskilled novice builders to design and construct their own inexpensive houses in inner London, and their method has lessons for anyone planning and building on the small scale. Age is no barrier – some Segal-style self-builders over sixty years old are now living in the houses they built with their own hands.

Segal, who died in 1985, and Broome learned over the years exactly what information the untrained builder finds useful, and what is either ignored or confusing. Anyone tackling a major alteration to their living space can learn from the Segal system's experience.

The Segal houses are similar to medieval timber-frame buildings. The key development is the use of modern, easily available standard materials throughout the building, from the framework of standard-section timber to the building boards which enclose the house. Standard materials save money, and those selected are easy for the unskilled to cut with ordinary hand power tools.

Wherever possible, boards are used in their bought size, saving effort and reducing the risk of mistakes. Accurate cutting is not crucial, since the junction of two boards will be covered by wooden battens. Simple nuts and bolts form

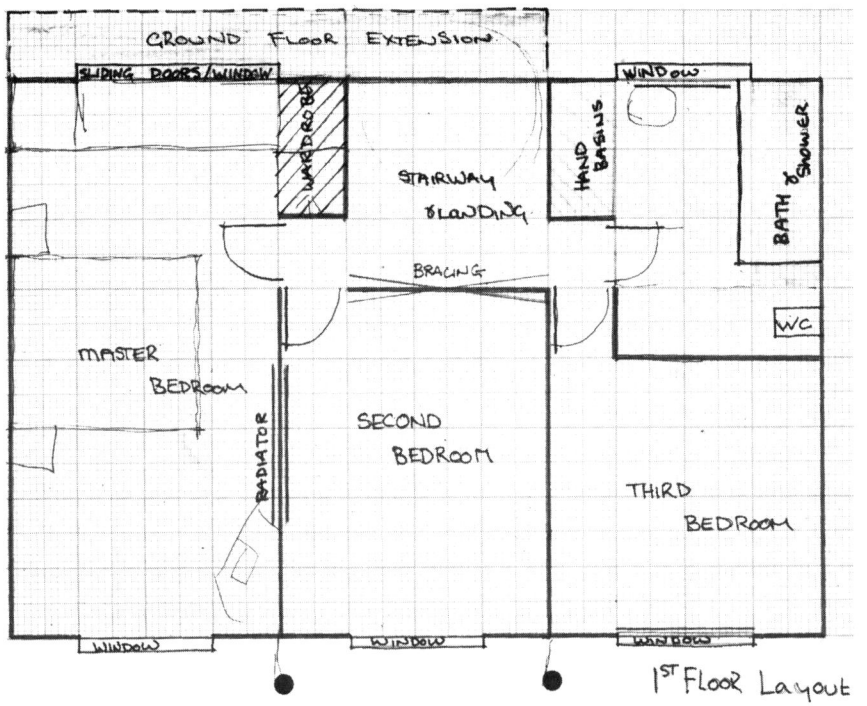

The plan (left) shows the layout of a Segal house. The frame is designed around this plan. The self-builder and architect design the house using a combination of layout drawings (below left) and simple models. Below, right: a page from the all-important schedule of materials, a complete shopping list of parts needed to build the house, running to about ten pages. This simplifies scheduling and cost control.

the fixings. Although this system is designed for the construction of complete houses, it is clearly adaptable to partial structures, when you are considering low-cost, easily built additions to an existing building.

The frame structure makes the houses admirably flexible. Walls, doors and windows can be moved quite easily whenever the occupants want a change of environment, and whole new rooms can be added without great effort. One occupant of the south London houses recently added a new room for a new child in the course of three weekends.

The system avoids complex and precise working drawings. Two or three freehand diagrams show the layout and structure, basically where the walls and openings will be. These are supplemented by diagrams of the standard joints in the construction, a list of materials needed for that particular house and a set of building instructions. It bears more than a passing resemblance to Meccano.

Wherever possible the architects, who are on hand to help throughout the whole process, demonstrate by example. They find that their main

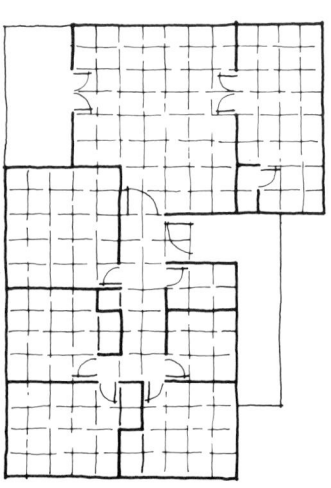

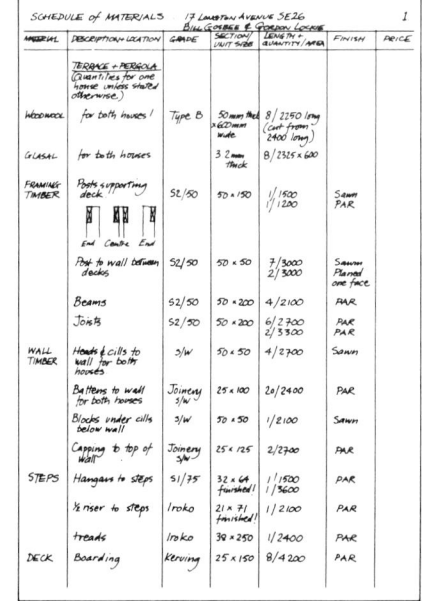

contribution is in getting people started. Once on site, the new builders learn from those who have been through it before.

Everyone attends a series of a dozen confidence-building evening classes at the start of the scheme. They are shown slides of both completed buildings and houses under construction, and shown how to progress from the initial plans and schedule to the finished house. 'It is all to do with self-confidence,' Jon Broome believes, 'and the most important thing is to get people confident with tools.' During the classes, therefore, the self-builders are taught how to handle the tools they will need to make the joints they will use. A course of evening classes could be beneficial to anyone altering their small apartment or house, reducing the risk of expensive on-site errors.

Models, the scheme's architects have found, are a valuable aid to non-builders, many of whom find it hard to visualise a finished three-dimensional building from two-dimensional drawings. The models consist of a wooden base with coloured perspex/plexiglass panels. The organization of the buildings on a modular pattern makes them particularly suitable for the use of models, but models will help the design of any small space, however complex, where the use of every available corner is crucial.

The interior of an early (1970) Walter Segal house at Yelling, England (right). The panel joints are covered by pine boards, an effect well suited to the plain wood flooring and furniture.

Written instructions have largely been abandoned, as people rarely used them. However, there is a written schedule of materials, which the architects prepare once the future occupiers have decided on the individual design of the house they will build. The schedule is an all-important, multi-purpose document, well worth drawing up, even if it means calling in an architect, if you are concerned about cost control.

The Segal schedule is basically a ten-page shopping list, itemizing every part used in the building, and giving its size, length and finish. It is used for calculating costs (which can be done very accurately before any materials are bought), for ordering materials and for checking them when they arrive on site. It also explains precisely where each part fits into the structure. The use of the schedule reverses normal building practice, in which the drawings are the key to the construction.

The self-builders are supplied with simple drawings, which they use mainly in the early stages of construction. Once the basic framework is erected, few people consult them. Some drawings nevertheless prove to be useful tools, particularly the detail diagrams showing how the parts fit together, which are used in conjunction with the step-by-step instructions.

The Segal system offers one great advantage for people fooled by plans, who end up with a building they dislike. Windows, doors and even walls can be repositioned with great ease. If you don't like them where they are, change them. That is a reassuring possibility.

Modern centre-pivot window; not in keeping with house; occupies room space when open; change for sash?

9in (225mm) solid brick wall. Plastered inside.

Original wood panel doors in goo condition. Could hinge on other side. Check fire regs – do they have to be self-closing?

Chimney breasts. Removal would create space, but will contain flues for fires downstairs. Do they use their fireplaces? Ask.

Wooden floorboards on 7 × 2in (175 × 50mm) joists.

The two rooms in the drawing on the right make up one floor of a real London terrace house (above). The illustration on pages 76-77 shows how a bathroom, kitchen, bedroom and living-room can be fitted into the 320 sq. ft (30 sq. m) available, making a liveable flat which does not fall foul of planning regulations. The process of planning begins with an assessment of the existing structure. Removing non-structural walls is messy but not difficult. Cutting away an existing chimney breast is a much more difficult job, but in this case we decided it was worthwhile in the back room because it allowed us to fit bathroom and bedroom in the width of the existing room. The chimney in the living-room has been left, although taking it out would have given more storage space.

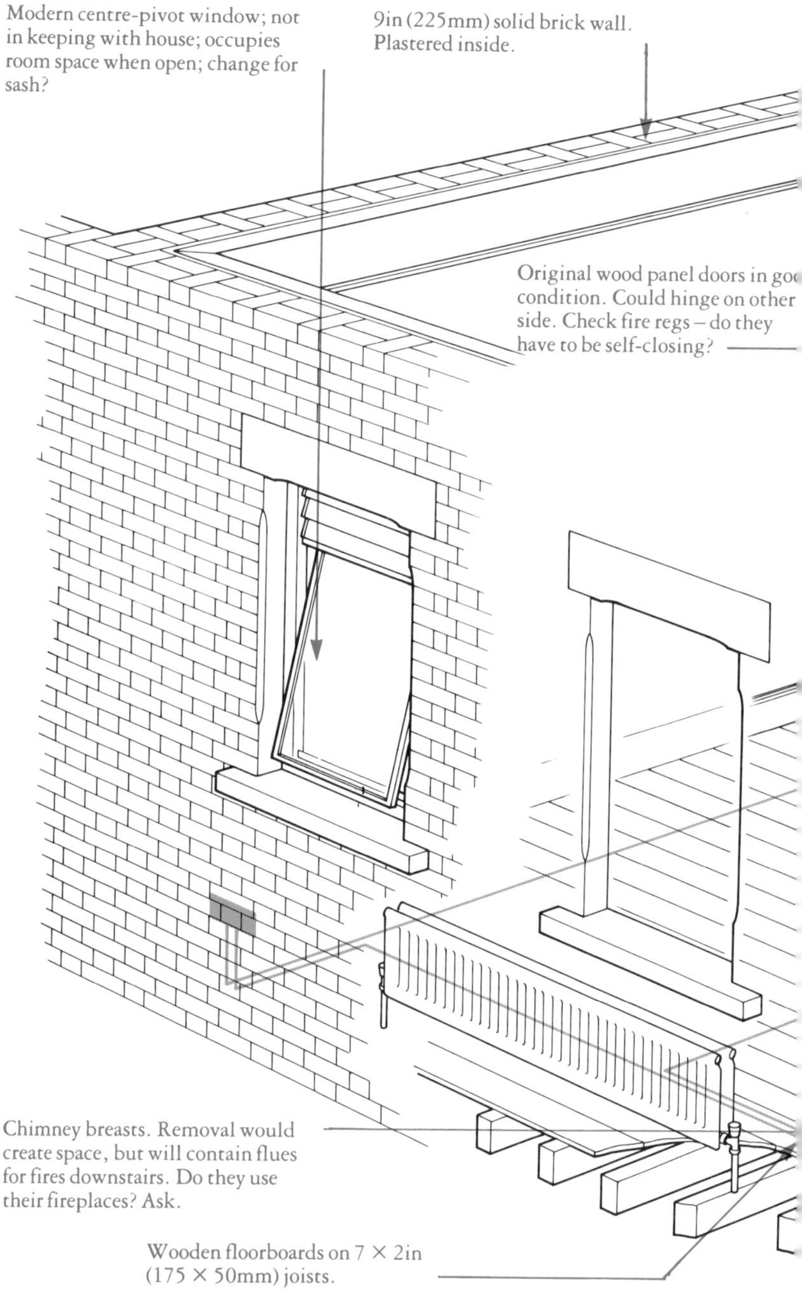

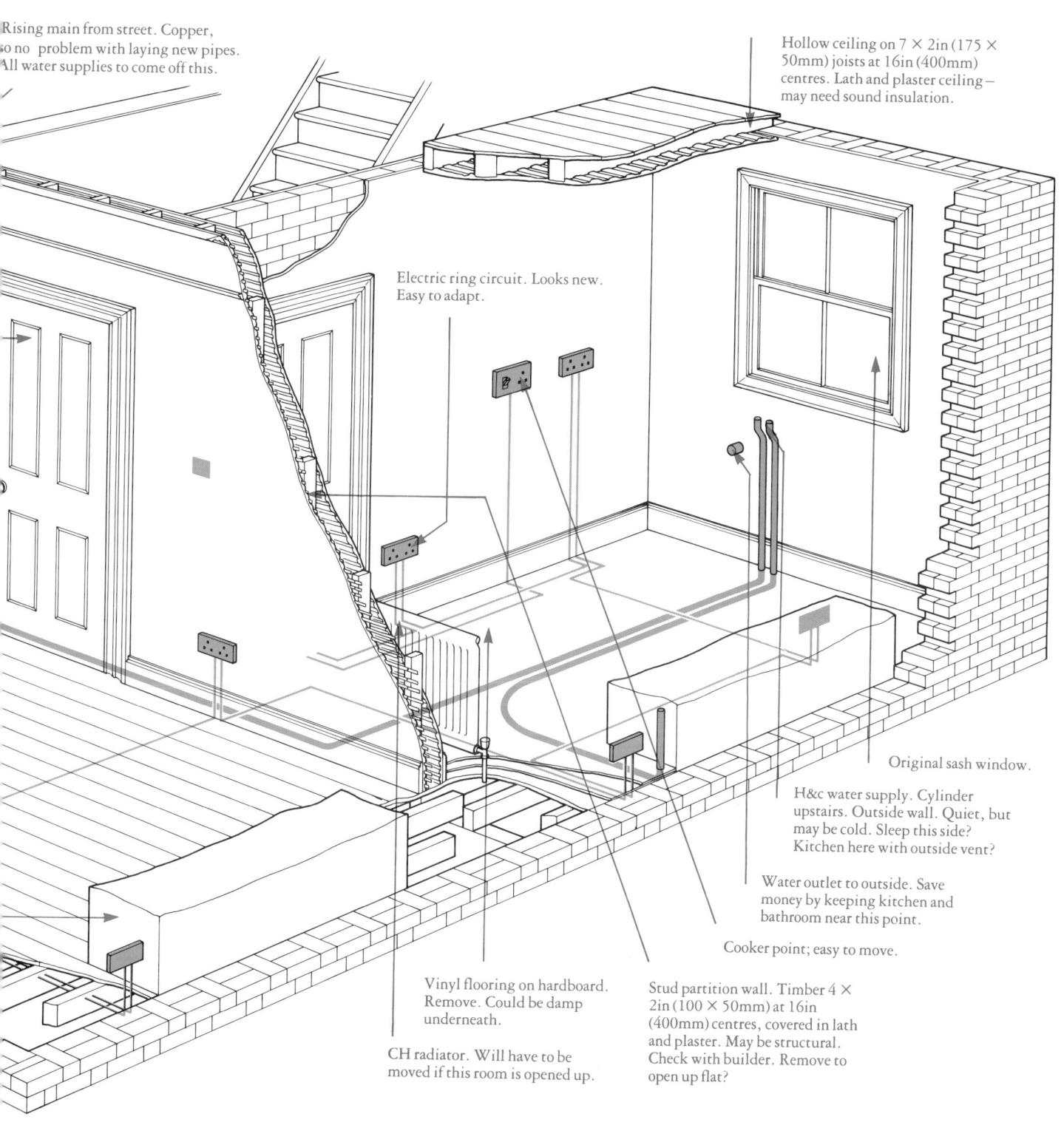

Rising main from street. Copper, so no problem with laying new pipes. All water supplies to come off this.

Hollow ceiling on 7 × 2in (175 × 50mm) joists at 16in (400mm) centres. Lath and plaster ceiling – may need sound insulation.

Electric ring circuit. Looks new. Easy to adapt.

Original sash window.

H&c water supply. Cylinder upstairs. Outside wall. Quiet, but may be cold. Sleep this side? Kitchen here with outside vent?

Water outlet to outside. Save money by keeping kitchen and bathroom near this point.

Cooker point; easy to move.

Vinyl flooring on hardboard. Remove. Could be damp underneath.

CH radiator. Will have to be moved if this room is opened up.

Stud partition wall. Timber 4 × 2in (100 × 50mm) at 16in (400mm) centres, covered in lath and plaster. May be structural. Check with builder. Remove to open up flat?

Good insulation makes sense in a small space. If part of your room is too cool, you'll avoid it. Sort out insulation before you work out your heating requirements; you should find you need a smaller heating system, which saves both space and money.

Covering the hot-water tank with a thick insulating jacket is the most cost-effective insulation measure, but draughtproofing your home will have a greater impact on your use of the space, by making cold corners more comfortable. At its most serious, draughtproofing can mean major jobs such as installing a draught lobby inside your entrance door, but there is unlikely to be room for one in a small space. Most measures are very cheap and easy to install.

Top priority goes to external doors and rattling sash windows, followed by casement windows and internal doors. There is a huge choice of patent sealing systems on sale. Self-adhesive foam strip is cheap but less durable than plastic 'V'tape, which will also accommodate gaps up to half an inch (10mm), a far greater range than foam. 'V'tape on the hinge side of a door can be supplemented by a flapseal on the top and lock sides, plus a brush device on the bottom of the door. The tape will also seal the gap where upper and lower sash windows meet top and bottom frame and where they meet each other in the middle.

Improvised materials such as papier mâché or a sawdust-and-glue mixture can be used to fill gaps in floorboards, while aluminium foil glued to the wall behind a radiator

Heat your room without using any of your valuable indoor space. The two side panels in the photograph (above) are sheets of glass backed by a black sheet which absorbs the sun's heat even on a dull day. Cold air from the room enters the system through the lower of the two vents in the drawing (opposite). It is warmed behind the panel and rises by natural convection, to re-enter the room, several degrees warmer, through the top vent. In cold weather, and at night, the vents can be closed. The positions of the vents are marked in the drawing by dotted lines. The section explains the construction of the system.
The central window in the photograph is a space-creating oriel window built into the Victorian house in Bristol, England, and used as a small greenhouse.

will reflect heat back into the room. Occupants of upper rooms may reflect, before insulating floors, that they are benefiting from the heating of the people below, since heat rises. This same physical fact makes it wise to insulate the upper floor of a two-storey dwelling first, to stop heat leaving through the roof.

Insulating the attic floor is a major money saver, but if you are short of space it could be wiser to use the attic rather than to insulate it. On the other hand, the cost of insulating can be recovered in a single winter, so if conversion must wait for finance or planning approval, insulate.

Temporary measures can save money and improve comfort. Some require no effort at all. Leaving your outside walls dirty, for instance, will keep the house warm – the white walls of the Mediterranean house or the space shuttle are designed to reflect heat. Other sensible if unattractive money savers include sheets of cling film stretched over window frames to act as instant secondary glazing. They require no fixing at all, though a blast with a hair drier can improve the system's looks by shrinking it tight. A sheet of clear rigid plastic is nevertheless prettier.

Secondary glazing is much cheaper than double glazing. The commonest form of double glazing is the curtain. This can be made more effective by a lining of mylar – a development of space research – or fixed at the top of the window with Velcro to reduce draughts.

Incidentally, extending the curtain rail on each side of a small window allows the curtain to be drawn completely free of the window during the day and creates the illusion of a larger window as well as increasing light levels in the room.

Some effective energy savers take no space in the house. Cavity-wall insulation is one obvious example. A solar collector on the roof also uses no interior space as it preheats the hot water supply. The system shown in the illustrations (left and right) uses the sun to heat air rather than water. This passive solar air collector, which is simple to construct, uses a pair of solar panels mounted remarkably unobtrusively on the front of the house (see photograph, left), where they look like windows. The front of the panel is in fact glass, with a black sheet behind which absorbs the sun's heat. Inside the house the lower vent can be opened to allow cool air to be drawn in and warmed as it rises behind the sun-heated panel. It emerges through the top vent several degrees warmer. This generates a convection current through the room. The system relies on the sun's light rather than direct sunshine and will therefore work even on dull days.

The 'Oriel' window in the centre of the photograph – which replaced a rattling and draughty sash window in the Victorian house – is another do-it-yourself job. It provides a small greenhouse and a platform at seat height. The window panels at the side are plastic, and they diffuse the morning and evening light, prolonging the day for the plants and people inside. Hinged window panels can isolate the greenhouse from the rest of the room.

The presence of plants is desirable in a well insulated room. They can lower the levels of some of the unpleasant fumes which accumulate in poorly ventilated spaces – carbon monoxide from smoking, nitrogen dioxide from gas cookers, formaldehyde from the glues used in plywood and particle board – which pollute our home air. Over-zealous draughtproofing can be dangerous. Human beings need fresh air to breathe. The lack of fresh air is traditionally a problem in the submerged submarine, where it leads to headaches and running eyes, and in the space shuttle, where there are no windows to open and seven bodies are constantly using up the oxygen. Oddly enough the shuttle's ventilation system has become a method of finding lost objects. In the weightless conditions they are all drawn inexorably to the extract ducts, where they wait for collection.

Ventilation is particularly important where you have open fires, as bad gases can accumulate fast and fires need constant oxygen. It is wise to leave at least the top of internal doors uninsulated.

A lightweight shutter can provide dramatically effective and simple insulation. It can be as simple as a 1in (25mm) sheet of expanded polystyrene/styrofoam covered with thin plywood and hinged to a batten screwed to the inside wall. No tough woodwork is needed, and it cuts the heat loss through the window by 90 per cent, as effective – and opaque – as a 9in (225mm) brick wall. It should be draughtproofed around its edges.

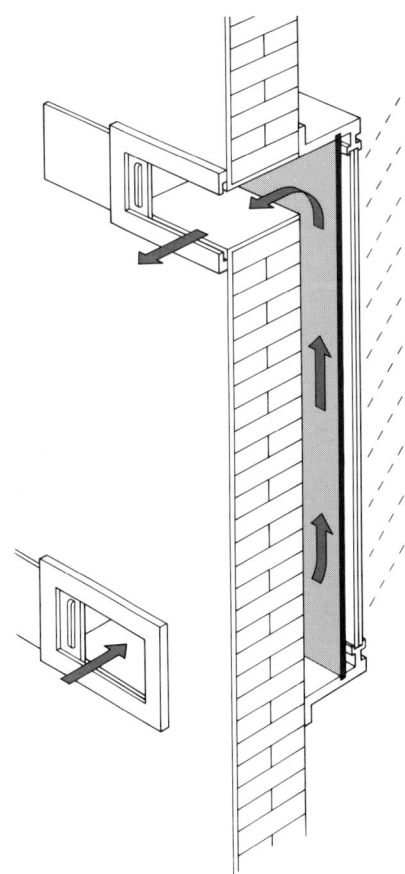

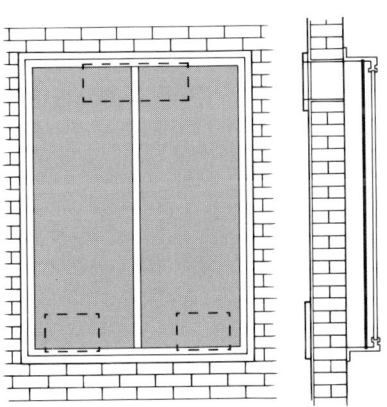

Crowded living conditions can look cosy in photographs, partly because the photograph does not show noise. Noise is one of the most wearing problems of life in a small space surrounded by high-decibel neighbours. Indeed, it is the most frequently reported cause of friction between neighbours. The walls in many modern houses offer no more than an illusion of privacy. Siting the parts of your space where you want peace as far as possible from walls shared with noisy neighbours can help, and sound insulation can make life more private, more comfortable and more relaxing. Submariners often feel irritated by the normal noise levels of life on land. The submarine is extremely crowded, but because the world is quiet under water, tension is low.

Sound-insulation measures can be depressingly greedy of space. Most of the techniques on display in a sound recording studio – such as padded walls and double doors, slate reflectors and box screens of rockwool – are very effective but consume too much space for use in small rooms. The efficient foam rubber wall-panels sold by suppliers of recording equipment are excellent if you can afford them.

Doors and windows are the priority points in your battle against noise. Noise often travels easily through entrance doors. Draught-proofing will reduce sound penetration without taking space, although it will also cut ventilation. Constructing an outside porch will further limit sound transmission.

Windows are the commonest entry point for sound. Bricking

Heath Robinson's exposition of the science of sound insulation in his illustration for the book How to Live in a Flat *('a resilient and noise-proof floor') incorporates two kinds of lightweight cellular material (footballs and wool) to absorb sound, and a three-skin ceiling. The sound which does reach the sleeper will mostly be coming through the walls.*

The drawings on the facing page show ways of cutting down the amount of noise which travels through partition walls. The two skins of plasterboard are mounted to the studs with spring clips, the studs are split down the middle, or a false third skin is added. All of these are ways of stopping the vibration caused by sound on one side being transmitted by the studs to the other.

them up is over-dramatic and may break planning regulations. Heavier glass helps, but adding a second window of heavy glass – with a gap of at least 6in (150mm) between the two – is much better. The fixing should be as airtight as possible, since the system is only as effective as its weakest point. Sound is moving air; where air can move, sound can travel. The new window will reduce ventilation, and air-conditioning may therefore become necessary.

It is relatively easy to stop high-pitched sounds by adding a new skin to walls and windows, with an air gap between the two, but the long wavelengths of bass sounds can leap a gap of several inches, and these are the ones which cause trouble between neighbours. The standard barrier to bass sounds is a room within a room. Where there is too little space for this, building a platform some 18-24in (450-600mm) high can help. The platform should have few contacts with the floor and these should be rubberized. The space created under the platform can be exploited for storage, and access to the storage space should be designed into the system.

Heavy curtains can be used as sound-absorbers over windows, doors and walls. A double layer of curtains with a 6in (150mm) gap between them is doubly effective, but uses a lot of space, although the gap can be used for book storage, for example.

Bass sounds travel through floor joists and drive neighbours insane. The problem of noisy floors can be sorted out by a few tons of sand

between the joists of wooden floors, but that could create a beach scene in the room below. Above weak ceilings the sand can be supported on chipboard/particleboard laid on battens fixed to the joists. Pushing mineral wool between the joists improves matters slightly, particularly if you lift all the floorboards, lay underlay over the joists, cover that with 2 x 2in (50 x 50mm) battens at 16in (400mm) centres, laid – but not fixed – at right angles to the joists. Nail the boards to these battens to make a floating floor. Seal the gaps between the boards and you have a reduction in both sound and heat movement.

Carpet underlay is a real barrier to sound; it contains air which cannot vibrate because it is trapped inside the foam rubber. Underlay can be glued to a wall, where its effectiveness is increased if it is wrinkled into a wave pattern to break up the sound. It looks ugly and should probably be covered up.

Bare brick or block walls can be made more soundproof by a coat of plaster. The next line of defence is the addition of a second wall skin. Resilient damping board is extremely good for this job, but all the joints must be well sealed if the treatment is to work. The new skin is most effective if it is fixed to the old wall – if possible on both sides – with sound-absorbing spring clips. One surprisingly effective wall technique takes up no space at all: when constructing a partition wall, simply saw a slot down the whole length of every stud to within an inch of the base. And in emergencies, use earplugs.

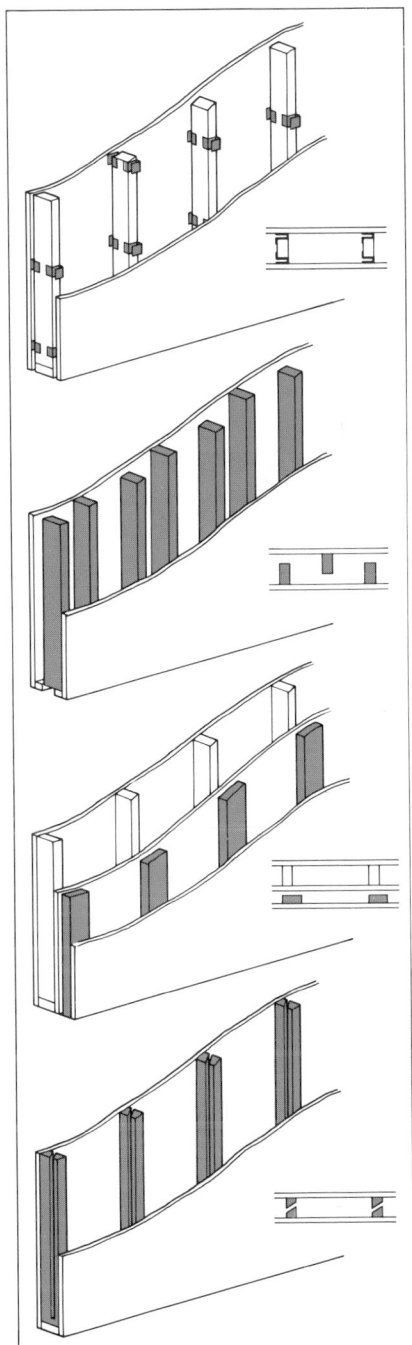

Minimalist furnishers may want to sit on the bare floor and would therefore appreciate draught-free comfort. Others will create dramatic and individual floors, seeing in their small space the opportunity to use labour-intensive techniques and expensive materials which would be too costly in a larger area. Whatever your choice, some general considerations apply.

Kitchens need floors which are easy to wash, as spills are most common and hygiene most important here. Non-slip floor surfaces will reduce the risk of accidents. Ceramic or quarry tiles make good-looking, easily mopped floors, but are expensive, cold and noisy, and they invariably get the better of dropped crockery. Vinyl and well sealed cork are cheaper, warmer, more flexible and cause fewer breakages. They are also easier to lay yourself. Because of the hard wear they will endure, plain wood boards or a hardboard/masonite covering on the floor must also be very well sealed for use in kitchens.

The risk of spills rules out deep-pile carpets in kitchens, but special carpet tiles are available with a proofed close pile and synthetic rubber backing. They are both warm and quiet, which can be a real benefit in small spaces where neighbours are close and tetchy. They are liked by tidy cooks, particularly if the kitchen is used for eating in or if young children play there while adults are at work.

Bathrooms are also subject to spills, wetter but cleaner than those that drop on the normal kitchen. Ceramic tiles are easily mopped, but vinyl is once again both warmer and cheaper. Mats used on smooth surfaces should have non-slip backings. Carpets make bathrooms warm and luxurious, but only a waterproof backing can stop them soon becoming sodden and unpleasant. Bathroom floors should be laid carefully so water cannot penetrate the covering and begin a damp attack on any wood underneath.

Even eating can be messy. An early solution was to strew the floor with rushes and replace them on holidays. Woven straw or fibre mats and luxury pile carpets can soon become ingrained with dropped food in the dining area. From the early eighteenth century, decorated washable oiled cloths were placed under the table, to be superseded by linoleum in the 1860s. Both linoleum and painted floorcloths are enjoying a revival. Painting your own floorcloth is a long job, but the effect can be stunning. The traditional method of manufacture was to apply several coats of size and paint, hanging the floorcloth up to dry between coats, before printing on the pattern. Today's hand-made cloths are often painted with *trompe l'oeil* marble and wood patterns, as were the floorcloths used by Queen Victoria.

Most people like to step on something warm, not necessarily the cat, when they get out of bed. Low quality carpet is suitable in rooms used only as bedrooms, as they receive little wear. A nineteenth-century treatment in bedrooms was to run strips of carpet around the bed over a painted and varnished wood floor. The twentieth century's wall-to-wall carpets make both sleeping and sitting areas feel warmer and look larger, particularly if plain unobtrusive colours are used. The use of the same fitted flooring – whether carpet or floorboards – also gives continuity to a series of linked spaces.

Squares of rush matting or the larger Japanese tatami mats can have the same unifying effect, but it can be difficult with these materials to arrange a precise fit in a given space, which may not be square. If you are aiming for the all-over effect, consider painting the surrounding floor in a colour to match the covering.

With continuous floor covering, small rugs can be strategically placed to take extra wear and to identify different areas within the room. When walls have been taken down to create more usable space and more light, the separate areas can be visually defined by their floor treatment. For example, the kitchen area can be tiled while the rest of the room has a wood or carpeted floor, with a warm rug by the sleeping space.

If walls are being erected to divide a large room, think about floors first, especially if wiring and plumbing are to be carried out, since the floorboards will probably be harder to lift when the new wall is in place.

Sanding the floor will also be harder when the space is divided and there are eight awkward corners rather than four. Hand sanders will

Floors of mosaic (like the second-century AD Roman example from Verulamium on the left) and of inlaid wood (the example below was made by the American artist-craftsman Wharton Esherick) are options for the patient and the skilled. The individual glass, stone or ceramic tesserae of which mosaic is made come in wonderful colours – the problem is laying them. Mosaic is heavy and must be laid on a solid floor, so it is usually only a ground-floor or apartment-block option. The apple-wood and walnut floor was laid in Esherick's Pennsylvania studio in 1941. In this handmade interior little is quite square, and all the surfaces are made with the same care. Such wooden floors can be laid over – or replace – existing boards.

be needed for edges and corners and should be used gingerly, as they can scar the floor. If possible, practise on a part of the floor which will be hidden. It really is worth taking care when applying the floor seal (over a coloured stain if this is wanted), lightly hand-sanding between at least three thinly applied coats, to give years of resilience.

Covering the floorboards with manmade boards, wood-block, parquet or carpet can alter the apparent shape of the space, since floorboards have the effect of exaggerating the length of the room in the direction they run. When laying new floors, consider the possibility of providing underfloor storage space.

Painting and stencilling, unlike sanding, are easier on smaller areas, as the end is always in sight. Special paints are available to take the battering they get on floors, but be prepared for heavily used areas such as doorways to need repainting before too long. The techniques are described in a number of how-to manuals which reflect the recent fashion for these traditional hand-painted finishes. The designs do not have to be traditional: paint can be applied in random flecks or splashes, and stencils can be blocks and triangles of colour inspired by this century's abstract paintings.

Modern paintings, or indeed Roman mosaics, can also inspire extraordinary use of vinyl or lino flooring. Use graph paper, to scale, and the ideas in, say, a constructivist painting or a Bridget Riley to design a geometric patterned floor. Cut it out in your choice of coloured lino or

vinyl and stick it down, following the manufacturer's instructions or the advice in the do-it-yourself books. If you feel nervous, do a trial run in paper first.

This treatment could be used to define an area of a room, set in the context of a single-colour floor. If you decide on a brand-new wood floor, look in one of the technical guides to wood properties published for the trade and available to the general public, such as the leaflets published by TRADA (Timber Research and Development Association) in the UK. These tell you the properties of various woods and their suitability for particular jobs.

Three-dimensional mosaic designs, such as the one in the patterned floor tiles of the café in the great Djemaa-el-Fna square at Marrakesh, Morocco (above), could be reproduced at home in linoleum or vinyl tiles. A far more ambitious project would be the reproduction of a full-sized painted floor cloth. In the nineteenth century, floor cloths were produced in lofty factories (right). A coarse woven canvas is stretched on a frame and sized to prevent the oil paint penetrating the canvas and making it brittle. It is then rubbed level with a pumice stone and painted on both sides with several coats of treacly oil paint. By rubbing down well between coats, durability is improved and a leather-like effect achieved. Unwanted or threadbare carpets can be turned over, painted and used as floor cloths.

Well-lit spaces feel larger. Increasing window size or adding new window openings exploits natural light and improves ventilation. Replacing ill-fitting windows will also reduce damp (which lowers temperatures and rots wood and decorations), draughts (which can make the space around the window too uncomfortable to use), and dust (which creates work).

With such major benefits, the temptation to convert the walls of your small space to glass is strong. Bear in mind that the increased heat gain through glass can turn the place into an unbearable greenhouse in the summer. These problems can be particularly serious in attic rooms. Overheating can be limited by placing the windows on the north or east sides of the building.

Planning regulations may also influence your window designs. As a rough guide, regulations often demand that the size of the window openings in habitable rooms must be at least one tenth of the floor area. This can be a problem if you are dividing a large room into two smaller ones.

Local regulations may also reinforce aesthetic considerations, banning the replacement of original windows with modern picture windows. Your despair at planning refusal should be tempered by the knowledge that tearing out the original windows will usually reduce the value of your property and deter discerning buyers. Modern windows are more acceptable at the side or back of the building.

Where possible, new windows should look as if they have always

Skylights do not disturb the outside appearance of a house.

been there. Styles, proportions and sizes should be carefully matched. Line up the heads and sills of new windows with existing ones. If this is not possible, line up the head rather than the sill.

The most acceptable replacement for a rattling, rotten, draughty, old-fashioned sliding sash window is normally another sliding sash. The top and bottom sections of the sash open independently, giving very flexible ventilation. Most

importantly, this type of window takes up none of your limited internal space when it is open, unlike pivoted or hinged windows. Horizontally sliding windows offer similar space economy. Louvered windows may be too insecure and cleaning them can be very laborious. The sash also allows you to use the window shelf for storage or display.

On upper floors, make sure that windows can be cleaned from the inside. Although a fixed skylight is the least expensive type to insert in a roof, and can be fitted by a competent do-it-yourself enthusiast, it may be impossible to clean. A pivoted one is therefore preferable. Covering a sloping skylight with curtains or blinds can be difficult. Some models incorporate a blind into the frame.

A dormer window creates more space in the attic, but is harder to install. Part of the roof will have to be removed. For structural reasons, it is unwise to fit a dormer over 4ft (1.2m) wide, to avoid weakening the roof to a point where extra support will have to be inserted. For aesthetic reasons, a pair of dormers, equidistant from the sides of the house, may be preferable to a single central dormer on the front of the house. Dormers can be effectively disguised by painting their frames the same colour as the roof. The frame pattern should match that on the existing windows.

On lower floors, the equivalent of the dormer is the bay or oriel window, popular around the world, from the old city of Jerusalem to modern Hong Kong (see page 38). Before choosing a simple replacement window, consider adding extra space by constructing a bay or balcony.

Increasing window sizes can reduce privacy and open up an unpleasant view. Translucent glass can solve both problems, cutting out the view but letting light and a feeling of outside space enter the room. Clear glass can be made semi-transparent by sandblasting it or spraying it with 'frost'. A partial solution comes with glazing bars, which have the effect of breaking up the view. A display of plants on glass shelves fixed in front of the windows has a similar effect.

Plants will reduce the amount of light coming into the room. If your problem is too much light in the room, louvered shutters can partially cover the window. Shutters are versatile window coverings. Outside shutters give privacy and climate control throughout the Arabian peninsula; indoor shutters are seen at their most refined in seventeenth-century Dutch houses.

Completely omitting shutters, blinds and curtains makes the room feel uncluttered, but provides no privacy and an easy passage for draughts to enter and heat to leave. Plain roller blinds look authentic even in old rooms. Manufacturers of blinds were already common in eighteenth-century London. They were popular because they used expensive cloth more sparingly than the curtains which were being fitted in the best houses after about 1725. Windows covered in curtains will appear larger if the curtain rail is extended on both sides of the window.

The method of fitting a new window varies with the wall construction (solid brick, block, cavity, wood-frame), but certain general principles apply. Carefully remove part of the wall to make a window opening; fit a lintel above the opening, with temporary supports; make good the opening, flush both sides; fit a sill, unless your window incorporates one; fix a wooden frame to hold the window precisely; set the window in the frame and make it weathertight.

Narrow-slatted Venetian blinds have increased the choice of window coverings. If your windows are recessed, the blinds should be hung in the recess rather than in front of it to make them less conspicuous.

When old windows are replaced, double glazing is a routine choice. However, it can be hard to find double-glazed windows in acceptable traditional patterns, and a secondary window fitted inside the room may be a better investment. It will also reduce noise penetration.

Ambitious do-it-yourselfers can increase light by creating a new window opening. An engineer or surveyor should first check that this will not weaken the wall – by being too close to a corner, for example – and that it will not contravene planning regulations. However small the window, the ceiling above it must be propped up during the work. Props can be hired, or a pair of 4 x 2in (100 x 50mm) vertical timbers wedged under a third spanning the joists.

Choose your window and make an opening large enough to take it by carefully removing bricks with a hammer and chisel. Fit a lintel above the window, extending at least 12in (300mm) either side. (This should be done as soon as possible, to prevent the wall moving.) A concrete base will be needed, and a sill if your window unit has no integral sill. Modelling a sloping sill can be hard. Formboards are nailed temporarily in position to hold the wet concrete. A wood frame is then nailed in the opening and flashed. From this point, follow the window manufacturer's instructions.

Colour and imagination transform a run-down London flat. The designers' approach and the techniques they used are described on pages 93-94.

LIGHTING

The car-aerial light by Ron Arad (right) offers one solution to the mobile-lighting problem. It can be rotated, raised and extended by remote control.

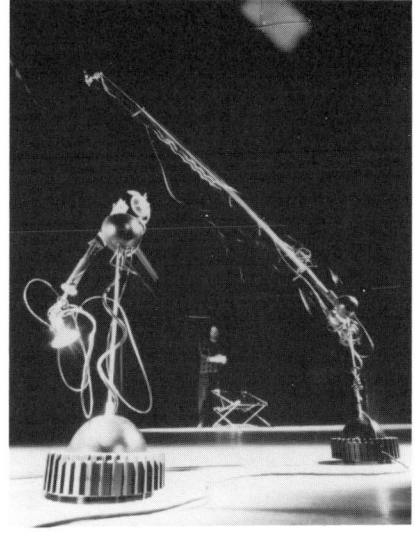

The centrepiece of architect Alessandro Ferrari's conversion of a Milan apartment (opposite; see also pages 95-7) is the multi-purpose, two-level service-block structure. The kitchen runs around two sides. Glass blocks provide a practical, easy-clean splashback in the kitchen and let light into the bathroom behind. On the platform above the kitchen and bathroom is the bed, raised slightly from the floor to improve air circulation and access. The storage around the platform is also designed for easy access. It is all above waist level, leaving the lower half of the platform open. You don't need a seven-foot-high closet to hang a shirt or jacket.

A stark, white, old-fashioned bath and hand-basin stand in the extraordinary bathroom of a Soho (London) flat (previous page; see also pages 93-4). Designers Simon Withers and Christos Tolera cut the cracks in the wall's fresh plaster using a craft knife, and filled them with pigment to achieve the look of instant decay. The 'marine rockery' is concrete pressed over a chicken-wire frame and coated with molten carnauba wax. A tray of sand behind the baseboard absorbs damp and no doubt attracts cats. The big cat on the bedroom floor gapes at a remarkable piece of decoration lit by a bare bulb dangling in the centre of the room. Paint was applied around the edge of the original panelling and worked towards the middle with a dry brush to give the aged look.

Lighting is one area of interior design where people are increasingly willing to borrow ideas – and even equipment – from sources outside the home. Fittings originally designed for use in offices and photographic studios and on construction sites are now commonly sold for home use.

Good lighting design is not simply a question of increasing the light level. An increase would no doubt make the space feel larger, but it can be very depressing to sit in a room which is so brightly and evenly lit that no vague areas remain. Your space may be small enough to light adequately with a single bare bulb dangling in the centre of the room, but thoughtful lighting can make the place feel both more spacious and more interesting.

The mathematical approach to lighting design can be extremely daunting to anyone unfamiliar with terms such as Lumens, Lux and Utilization Factors. Fortunately, technical knowledge is not at all necessary

A practical test can take the place of experience. Gather together as many portable lights as you can, and take them into your space on a dark evening. Try them in various positions – shining upwards, downwards from the ceiling, sideways along the wall. Use them at various heights in the room, from floor level to ceiling. Try placing uplighters behind furniture or plants. Try them singly and in various combinations. Notice the effect when you light the room indirectly, by bouncing light off walls and ceilings. Bright walls tend to make the room feel larger.

The theatre is a limitless source of lighting ideas, and an old theatrical trick can provide you with an instant 'wall', a flexible and reversible alternative to dividing the space by solid walls. Hang diaphanous gauze across the room – light it from the front and it's opaque, light it from behind and it becomes transparent. Walls are, of course, far more effective during the day!

Theatrical-lighting designers also exploit the colour of lights. Few humans look at their best under green light, as we learn from the horror movie, and red lighting spoils the appetite of the submarine crew. Red lighting is used at night to allow the captain to see through the periscope into the night outside, and it makes the food look an appalling grey colour. These extreme examples are relevant, since the objects in your home space will look very different under the two basic types of lamp on

LIGHTING

The diagram below shows how the cone of light from a spotlight expands and the number of lux (the unit used to measure illumination) decreases with distance. Most manufacturers include such diagrams in their catalogues. Lux levels which are recommended for typical situations are – conversation and relaxation: 50-100; reading for any length of time: 500-1000; fine detailed work (sewing for example) 1000-2000. The eye's needs change with age – someone under forty typically needs only half the light someone over fifty-five needs. Much light is reflected. Light walls need less powerful lights to achieve the same levels of illumination.

offer – cool fluorescent lighting and the warmer tungsten, whose warm tones recall the candle and the fireside, lighting sources which may have their place in your space. By careful mixing of the two types, you can create different feels in the room. Where several activities take place in the same space, flexible lighting is a good idea. Dimmer-switches are one simple and inexpensive way of changing the mood of a room through lighting. Controlling the various lights in a room by independent switches also increases flexibility.

Greater flexibility comes with portable lamps. Besides table lamps, standard lamps and uplighters, remember the classic Anglepoise and other adjustable-arm lights. Together with clip-on lamps which can be attached to a shelf or desk top, these could form the core of your lighting scheme.

It is particularly important in a small space that wires should not be trailing around the room waiting for someone to trip over them in the confined space. Make sure you have enough electrical sockets to accommodate your lamps. If you are short of sockets and don't want the disruption or expense of rewiring,

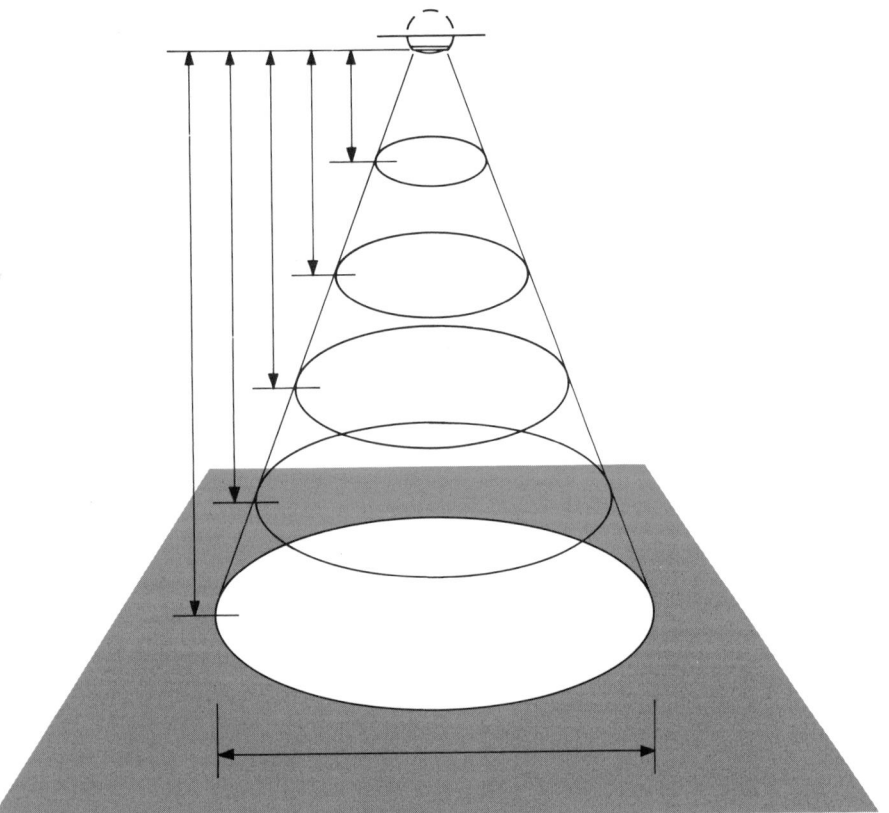

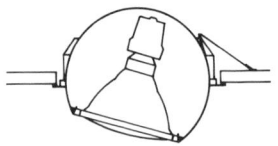

m	36°	Lux
1	0.65	3100
2	1.3	780
3	1.9	340
4	2.6	190
5	3.2	120

m	28°	Lux
1	0.50	2500
2	1.0	630
3	1.5	280
4	2.0	160
5	2.5	100

you may be able to replace single socket outlets with double ones; this is normally a simple job.

Decide what you are going to do in the space before you decide how to light it. Fluorescent lighting is useful in a kitchen, but harsh in a bedroom. In the kitchen, where sharp knives are wielded, good lighting is essential. Fix lights under wall-mounted cabinets to light up your work surfaces. A strip light could be fitted in the unused space over the window.

In the bedroom, take a tip from the airlines. Directional spotlights are mounted above the seats to allow one passenger to read without disturbing the person trying to sleep in the next seat. A similar arrangement will ensure harmony in a double bed. A principle borrowed from the refrigerator can also improve bedroom life: inside your closets, fix a light operated by a pressure switch, so the light comes on when the door opens.

Safety is the crucial concern in the bathroom, where the lethal mixture of water and electricity threatens life. Use no normal pendent lights, no switches except ceiling-mounted and cord-operated switches, and run no lights from power points. Make sure there is a light in the shower — a waterproof industrial light will do the job safely.

For safety reasons, you need good lighting on stairs and in halls, particularly in places occupied by old people, who need at least twice as much light as the middle-aged. Safe lighting is particularly important in confined spaces, where accidents can easily happen.

A careful choice of radiators can maximize free wall space and will affect the look of a room (see also page 96). The photograph (above) proves how wide a selection is on the market today, from the dumpy traditional radiator to sleek modern models. Do not leave the buying decision to your plumber. A professional can help you decide how much heating your room requires. Computers have refined the old rule-of-thumb calculations to determine the heating needs of domestic spaces. In the pre-computer era, calculations were usually applied only to large commercial spaces. Now certain radiator suppliers will work out the sums for even the smallest homes, where central heating may not be the most cost-effective heating system. This information can save money and space — rule-of-thumb methods often exaggerate needs.

It is wise to heat your small space well, since people tend to avoid cold areas, and you can't afford any wasted spaces.

One of the few major advantages of living in a small space is the relative ease and cheapness of heating it. The tiny living space in the traditional narrow boat, for example, is heated only by the same small coal-fired stove which heats the water and cooks the food. There was never any shortage of coal, since the boats would often be carrying forty-five tons of coal in the hold. Few small homes have a hold, and the need to store bulky fuel supplies usually makes fires burning coal or oil a poor choice for heating small spaces.

A winter spent on the canals in a narrow boat soon proves the importance of proper insulation. In an uninsulated boat the temperature difference between the water-cooled floor and the ceiling can easily be 30°F (17°C)!

Efficient insulation can mean you need fewer heating appliances to keep the space warm, and this in turn saves space. Tiny, well insulated spaces may need no heating at all; the heat of your own body may keep it warm. The homeless in London's garment district sleep in the tough coffin-like cardboard boxes used for the transportation of fabric rolls and thrown out each evening by the area's clothing manufacturers. An occupied box can warm up fast, and there is consequently some competition for sound boxes in the early evening.

The amount of heating you need varies with the type and exposure of the building as well as with its size and the level of insulation. There are rules of thumb used by many heating installers to calculate heating requirements in any space. These are generally based on floor area or room volume, and can be very simple. For example, room-volume-in-cubic-feet multiplied by 1.5 is said to give the number of watts needed to heat a room. More refined calculations are used for large non-domestic spaces where installation and running costs are much higher. Computer programmes now apply the same sophisticated methods to domestic situations.

High installation and maintenance costs can mean that a central-heating system may not be the most economical choice for a small space. Moreover, the boiler and water tanks needed for the system can also occupy a lot of room, although small wall-hung and balanced-flue boilers have reduced the scale of the problem. Nevertheless, many home-owners choose central heating simply because it increases the value of the property.

Wall-mounted heaters can be very unobtrusive, but any heating appliance can eat up valuable wall space. Modern radiator design has improved matters. Many modern radiators are much taller than they are long, leaving more horizontal wall space free. Some can even be used as room dividers. Modern electric storage heaters are also much more compact than their bulky predecessors.

Individual gas or electric heaters are more expensive to run than

British airmen with electrically heated clothing test equipment before a bombing raid during the First World War. It is cheaper to keep the body warm than it is to heat the whole room. The Japanese traditionally dressed warmly in winter, and used small containers of burning charcoal to keep themselves warm.

central heating, but low installation costs make them a good choice for small spaces. Plan for heating water as well as space, for instance by combining a gas fire with an instantaneous multipoint water heater.

The choice of appliances is wide. Timers and thermostats – major traditional advantages of central heating – are now freely available on individual gas and electric heaters. This means the heaters can be programmed to switch on and off at any given time or temperature. There are heaters for specific jobs. An electrically heated towel rail, for instance, may be sensible in a small bathroom, since towels have to be hung somewhere. The same room

could use a small fan heater with an integral electric shaver socket or light.

Portable heaters give you desirable versatility, but they can create problems in a confined space. Heaters burning kerosene or bottled propane will often cause condensation, as they can generate almost a gallon of water for every gallon of fuel burned. Such heaters demand good ventilation. Heaters should never be positioned where anyone could trip over them, nor should they be burning near curtains or furniture. Guards should be used on all fires, and if children or old people are using the space, the guard should extend well beyond the fire itself. Nursery guards which clip to wall brackets are sensible if unattractive. Just in case disaster strikes, be sure you find space in the home for a fire extinguisher.

More energy is used worldwide in the effort to keep places cool than to heat them up. Effective air-conditioning may therefore be more important to your comfort in a small space than good heating. Obviously it is crucial to remove cooking smells efficiently, and a cooker extractor fan, perhaps supplemented by a second fan, will do the job. The experts in keeping living spaces cool are people living in hot climates. Look, for example, at traditional housing design in the Caribbean. Without air-conditioning plant, the occupants keep cool by creating air currents through the building and protecting the interior from the sun by awnings which keep the building in the shade. Saharan nomads use similar systems.

BUILDING LAW

Local planning and building laws will almost certainly affect your designs if you are changing or extending your space. They cover what you can build and how you can build it, and they can be extremely irritating and impenetrably complex at times. It is worth remembering that they are there to protect your own health and safety.

The rules change from year to year and from place to place. They usually apply differently in houses and apartments.

The best source of local information on the law is the local agency that administors the Uniform Building Code, usually the Department of Buildings. Their inspectors will look at your plans and tell you whether they are likely to comply. Some even publish guidelines for non-builders.

The New York City Uniform Building Code forbids any alterations without permission, although work that "maintains" what already exists does not require approval. Thus you cannot make a bedroom in an attic where none existed previously, knock down walls inside a building, install a bathroom, or build a terrace without filing plans. You, your builder, or your architect will have to submit drawings for approval before work begins, and inspectors 'may enter at all reasonable times' both during and after construction. Application fees in New York City are based on the total cost of your alteration; in 1988 the city charged $55 for the first $1000 spent, $10 per $1000 for the next $4000, and $5 per $1000 thereafter.

The regulations are particularly strict on 'habitable rooms' that is bedrooms, living rooms, dining rooms, and kitchen-breakfast rooms. The Uniform Building Code specifies ceiling heights of at least 7ft 6in (2.3m) except in bathrooms, halls, kitchens, and basements, which can be as little as 7ft (2.1m) high. New Yori City laws, however, stipulate that all rooms must be at least 8ft (2.4m) high, with windows at least one-tenth the area of the floor space.

Habitable rooms and kitchens in New York City must have either adequate artificial ventilation or an area of ventilation to the outside that is at least one-tenth of the floor area. However, dining bays less than 56sq. ft (5.2sq. m) are required to have one window that is at least one-eighth the area of the floor. The top of this vent must be at least 68in (1.8m) from the ground. The vent is usually an opening window, but the fact that external doors count in the calculation can simplify plans.

A rule certain to frustrate New York's Peeping Tom population dictates that city apartment windows be at least 30ft (9.1m) away from neighboring apartment buildings. No rules restrict the distance between windows and the street. The light or ventilation of a room, public hall, or stairs cannot be decreased without approval. While not normally considered habitable rooms, alcoves that open off a room are not part of a lawful cooking space, and are at least 7 × 10ft (2.1m × 3m), must be separately lighted and ventilated.

You will probably not be allowed to have your bathroom opening off a kitchen, and if there is no artificial ventilation in the bathroom, there must be an opening window whose area is at least one-tenth the area of the floor space.

The regulations on stairs are especially tricky. The tread (the flat part) and the risers (the step height) must be uniform in any one flight, with a tread of at least 9½in (240mm), and risers not more than 7¾in (200mm) high. New York City building authorities outline a rather bizarre formula whereby the inches of the tread multiplied by the inches of the riser must be at least 70 and at most 75. You can often avoid these complex problems in attic conversations by using a loft ladder or metal spiral staircase.

The problems and costs of becoming involved in the planning process can tempt people to ignore the law. This is not wise, for practical rather than moral reasons. If your neighbours complain about your works, or a roving building inspector spots signs of construction and decides to investigate, you may be forced either to restore the building to its original condition or to follow the law to the letter. This can be expensive, for in addition to unplanned-for construction costs, violation in New York carries a misdemeanor penalty of $500 or 30 days in jail or both for the first offense. Failure to remove the violation may result in a $1000 fine or 6 months in jail or both.

It may be possible to negotiate a relaxation of certain regulations if you discuss your plans with the authorities before you start building, but negotiations should always precede *any* physical alterations of the space.

A LONDON CONVERSION

These pages show an approach to the conversion of an existing building. The problem was to fit a self-contained one-person apartment – with the possibility of accommodating a second person – in one floor of a standard London terrace house. The original structure is illustrated on pages 58-59. Many of the ideas incorporated in the design are inspired by people, places and approaches covered in this book.

In the early stages we worked out what activities were going to take place in the flat and where they should happen (see pages 89-90), concentrating on all the things which it would be difficult to change at a future date, such as the position of all the fixed equipment. For example, the bathroom, kitchen and laundry are all close to the present water supplies and drainage, which saves time and money. Many details – including decoration – were left to be decided as the job progressed.

We used a combination of a measured floor plan roughly drawn on squared paper, sketches of our ideas and annotated photographs to work out the design (see pages 46-54).

Fitting kitchen, bathroom and bedroom into the existing kitchen meant compact solutions were crucial. Removal of the bulky chimney breast in the kitchen increased available space; removal was impossible in the front room. Space was further increased by the construction of an outside balcony inspired by the illegal models in

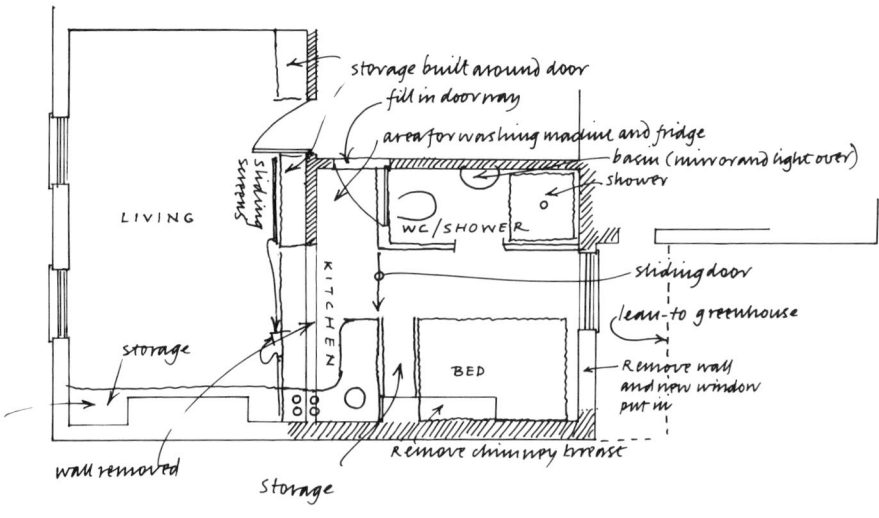

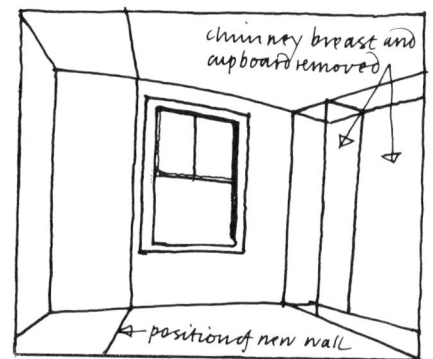

A plan, drawn up on graph paper, and a photograph used as a basis for sketches of intended changes.

76

Hong Kong (page 38) and the oriel window (page 60). The apartment was opened up by removing the partition wall and replacing it with a new screen wall with linked storage around the entrance door. A two-part sliding screen of translucent blue plastic with narrow corrugations can separate the kitchen/bathroom/bedroom from the living-room. This is influenced by both traditional Japanese ideas (pages 17-19) and Laurie Hawkinson's Kruger loft (page 26). The windows in the front room — which were modern centre-pivoted additions — were replaced with sliding sash windows, more in keeping with the original building; they also save internal space as they do not swing (pages 67-70). Windows are covered by narrow-slatted venetian blinds.

Storage space is necessarily limited. The area behind the bed is the major walk-in storage space, separating the bed from the kitchen and containing the sliding door. This structure also contains hangers on sliding racks above drawers, shoe racks and industrial shelving. The inside surface of the door is also exploited (pages 116-117) to hold brooms etc. A wall of storage, covered in mirror, is built into the living-room.

There was no room for a platform bed under this low ceiling. Our solution was a combination of Lawrence of Arabia's bed (page 25) and Shaker ideas of cabinet-making (pages 20-21). The use of wood in the bed/chest influenced the choice of materials in other parts of the apartment.

Flooring (pages 64-66) in the

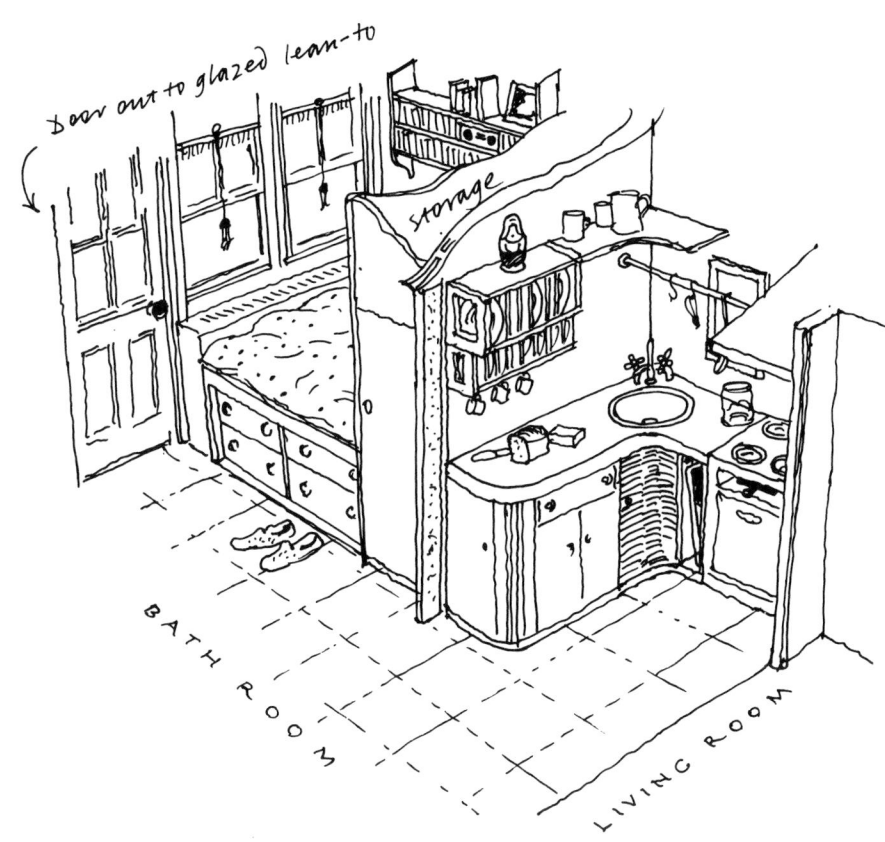

A sketch of the layout for bedroom and kitchen areas. Drawing from above often makes it easier to show how things will fit together.

bathroom, bedroom and kitchen is sealed cork tiles. Edges will be well sealed to avoid seepage. Tiles would be cold in the bedroom and brittle on the springy wood floor.

The kitchen is tiny. It has a plate rack (page 100) designed to fit the space available. A small fridge/freezer stands over an equally compact washing machine, which is plumbed in and linked to the

pipework in the adjacent bathroom. Heating is by the existing central heating system, with some radiators removed, others added. Improved insulation and precise calculations (page 73) mean that a smaller boiler can be used.

There is not much furniture. A solid table provides both eating and working surfaces. There are four good-quality folding chairs (pages 126-127) and a sofa for reading and relaxing which can double as a bed (pages 122-125). The video and audio equipment (page 119) is on a mobile trolley.

HOMES OF THE POOR

The Ulster cottage (left) and the shack (opposite) show different responses to the problems the poor face when they come to build. The cottage is a traditional building which makes no reference to the houses of the prosperous. The plastered wattle chimney canopy, the deep window reveal and the bed recess are features arrived at over a long period of time and conservatively copied.

The shack on Bequia, one of the Grenadines, West Indies, on the other hand, has an imitation cast-iron lace balcony and probably reuses old joinery. It certainly has an oil drum – one of the most versatile components industrialized countries put in the way of the third world – recycled as a water butt.

The unimproved English cottage was small and uncomfortable. Even the most romantic modern city-dweller looking for a rural weekend retreat would reject the gloomy mud cottages and the sunken one-room houses which could still be found in the west of England a hundred years ago.

The one-room cottage, sometimes with an added lean-to at the back, was the standard accommodation for England's rural labourers from the Middle Ages to the eighteenth century. There would be no cavity walls and no damp-proof course, so the cottage suffered from condensation and rising damp. Condensation and damp were the only running water, and an outside privy was usually the only sanitation. The stone flags, bricks and quarry tiles, which were an improvement on the original bare earth floors, were cold to the feet.

This unsatisfactory state of affairs was reflected in books of nineteenth-century cottage designs (Prince Albert himself did some) which encouraged more wholesome accommodation for the rural poor. The romanticization of the cottage coincided with mass movements of people to the growing industrial towns. The industrial versions – often terraces of back-to-backs in the shadow of pits or factories – were extremely depressing. They were tiny, overcrowded, two-storey, two-room houses, sharing their back wall with another identical house, and typically standing in rows of ten. Drainage was as absent as through-ventilation.

As the workers were increasingly housed by local authorities, their abandoned country cottages were bought by the wealthy, extended, made pretty, and turned into desirable houses (often second

homes for town dwellers).

Modernization can make something of the originals, but it would be romantic to think of rural and industrial workers' houses as being anything but substandard. They were also crowded. The cottage which now serves a couple at weekends began as the sole dwelling of a large family, and was often shared with a cow. The single man would probably live in his employer's house, a practice which continues today.

They did however incorporate features which are relevant to small-space living, like thick walls with deep, small, window openings. Cottages look inward. One argument is that if you were working outside all day, the last thing you wanted when you came home was a view. The cost of joinery and glass further restricted windows. The window area of a small flat today is often best kept small for other reasons. Wall space is valuable. You need it to put furniture against, and to hang things on. Once the basic needs of light and ventilation have been met, extra glazing is a luxury.

Glass doors, or half-doors with a glazed upper portion, are one way of getting light into refurbished cottages which is also appropriate in small conversions. Cupboards in the thickness of walls (see page 30) are another way of getting double use out of walls.

Cottages have low ceilings (lower than head height before the sixteenth century), often with uncovered beams. When the ceiling is within reach, things can be hung from it. You do not need to go as far as hanging strings of onions and hams. Kitchen implements, for example, can be hung within reach, but high enough not to bump heads.

The early cottage would be sparsely furnished. A trestle table, stools, bench, cupboard and bed would be normal and provide a good guide for minimal furnishing today. To save space, furniture such as beds, benches and cupboards would be built in rather than freestanding.

The cluttered look of cottage interiors is partly due to an accumulation of tools and ornaments, but it is also an effect of so much being stored in open view. The dresser is the obvious case, but delft racks, coat hooks, butchers' hooks, nets and racks — and the jars, crocks, tins and boxes which are stored on them — allow the workings of the house to be seen.

The 'clean' look of modern design, like the 'clean' look of

modern engineering, is a cover-up job. The working parts are put underneath a smooth shell.

Another feature of cottages is the central position in the kitchen (which is often the main living-room) of the cooking range. Before the invention of the range the fireplace occupied this position. Gathering services together keeps the plumbing and wiring tidy. It also gives a centre to the room — 'focus' is the Latin word for 'hearth' — and makes it easier to separate functions in an area which is used for both cooking and living. The inglenook seating built within the area of the fireplace was one kind of room within a room, the box bed

another. Modern versions of them can work well.

Miners', millworkers' and artisans' dwellings, which tend to be mass-produced to mean standards, have less to offer in the way of ideas. They are, however, a substantial part of the housing stock, particularly in the UK. One temptation is to simplify them by knocking rooms together. This should not be done lightly. Unless you are living on your own, and intend to continue that way, think of how you really live: do both — or all — of you really want to listen to the television at the same time? Do you want the telephone in the same room as everything else?

One possible bonus of bringing a small nineteenth-century house up to scratch is a big bathroom. There is often no room big enough to divide, so the original smallest bedroom is converted. It can work very well – the sheer size is a luxury, and laundry and linen storage can be incorporated, not to mention piped music and a library.

In spite of the chocolate-box image and high price of the country cottage today, its history places it much closer to the new shanty towns built around the developing world's major cities. Both rely on locally available building materials, whether corrugated iron and cardboard or the 16ft (4.8m) timbers which supported the medieval one-room English cottage. Only after the arrival of cheap transportation and the mass-production brick kiln in the mid nineteenth century were local materials replaced.

Both types of building begin as single-room dwellings, and both are simple to extend by building on new rooms when people can afford them. In the modern low-income third-world house, construction frequently takes place over twelve years.

Although the authorities often consider such housing undesirable, largely because they show a face of corrugated iron and other 'unofficial' materials to the street, the occupants take great pride in the achievement of having built their own house. It seems that you gain much more than space by self-build.

Like the medieval cottage, the self-build house in the third-world city doubles as a working space. It is interesting that however great the pressure on space, people are very reluctant to build over the land behind the house, which they use for private activities, growing fruit and vegetables, keeping livestock, cooking and washing. When construction is complete, the corrugated iron may come down, revealing a carefully decorated face.

When industrialization brought great numbers of people into cities, new building types – the mass-produced industrial equivalent of the country cottage – emerged. The infamous back-to-backs, like those in Leeds (below, left) were essentially two rows of farm labourers' cottages slammed hard against one another. With no through ventilation, and shared lavatories, they were a brutal expression of economic forces: Bradford byelaws forbade their construction as early as 1860. The cottage plan type is so basic that it seems inevitable in such very simple houses.

The shotgun house (below) – a building type found in the American South and Haiti – proves that this is not the case. Each house is one room wide and several rooms deep. Each room opens into the next, and the house has a front-facing gable. J.M. Vlach argues that the type can be traced back to West Africa, and that 'core cultural values concerning the appropriate use of space survive as a hidden heritage in spite of the hardships of slavery'.

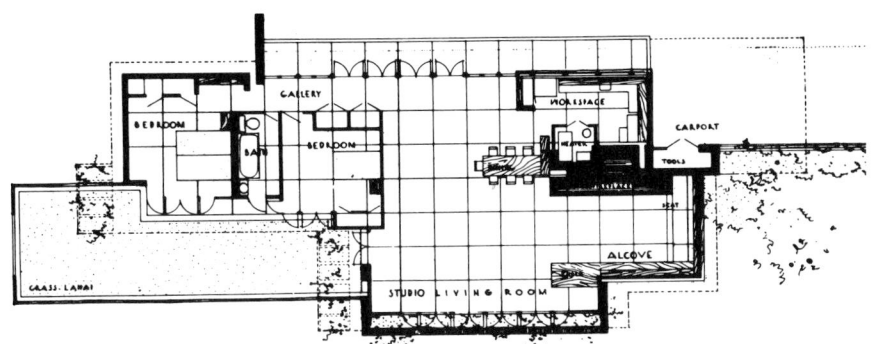

During the first half of this century modern architects made grand and often arrogant statements about the way people should live. Some of the architecture which grew out of this theorizing, in particular the minimum standard high-rise flat, is now generally regarded as disastrous. However, it was the modernists of the twentieth century who first made fitted kitchens, built-in furniture, and open planning standard items. Things which are now taken for granted were the lasting contribution of modern architecture to domestic planning. It is worth looking at their origins, and seeing how well the old masters of modernism handled them.

The American architect Frank Lloyd Wright built a number of houses for clients who were not rich, and developed the idea of the 'Usonian House', something to replace the 'expedient houses built by the million, which journals propagate and the government builds'.

In 1953 an exhibition house by Wright was put on show in New York, and the magazine *Architectural Forum* said that many Americans could now belatedly see '... suggestions first made in 1900 when his houses embodying the same principles first appeared on the prairie outside Chicago. Here for the first time in the Architecture of the West the human scale in building proportion appeared with the open plan.'

In the East, of course, things were different, as we have seen (pages 17-18), and the Japanese example meant much to Wright. The Jacobs house

Frank Lloyd Wright's plan of the Goetsch-Winkler house in Michigan, USA. It cost $9500 when it was built in 1939, and shows many features typical of Wright's Usonian houses, such as the built-in furniture, the kitchen backing on to the fireplace, and the single living space with glass doors opening on to terrace and garden, minimizing the separation of inside and outside.

of 1937 was planned on these principles. It saved money by having a carport rather than a garage, underfloor heating rather than radiators, indirect lighting rather than light fixtures. 'Furniture, pictures and bric-a-brac,' Wright wrote, 'are unnecessary because the walls can be made to include them or *be* them.' He wanted no painting (the woodwork is oiled) and no plastering (brick is left bare). The Jacobs house is planned around a core containing the cooking and bathing areas. There is a built-in dining area, and each bedroom has a wall of closet space. The kitchen is fitted.

What did Wright think was essential? 'A big living-room with as much vista and garden coming in as we can afford ... living-room tables built in and a quiet rug on the floor. Convenient cooking and dining space. The kitchen organized so that it is naturally ventilated.' Higher ceilings and top ventilation in kitchens made them into natural chimneys, drawing cooking smells

out and not letting them drift into the open living areas.

Wright was designing small houses, not flats, and assumes that the surrounding landscape will be part of the plan. But principles underlying his small open-plan houses have become part of the common vocabulary of all modern design. They went along with a view of the good life which valued simplicity, lack of clutter, light, efficiency and economy. They are the opposite of the rural-nostalgic interiors which seem to be the current interior-of-choice in the UK. But even those with nostalgic tastes will find Wright's plans repay a careful look, unless you plan to throw out the stainless steel sink and the central heating and have the electricity disconnected. Wright was the one great architect of the twentieth century to put many of his best ideas into individually planned, small, reasonably cheap houses. He also thought a little more about people and how they live than many of his peers.

In 1924 another quite different kind of modern house was built in Utrecht, Holland, by Gerrit Rietveld, for (and in collaboration with) Mrs Truus Schroeder. She lived there until her death in 1985. Like Frank Lloyd Wright's houses, it has built-in furniture, simple shapes, uncluttered surfaces, and big windows. It is famous as a pioneering building, one which suggests all the hopes of early modern architecture – it was an architect, Colin St John Wilson, who once called it 'the youngest house in Europe'.

Whereas Wright built on generous suburban plots, this house is urban. Even when it still stood on the edge of town it was inward-looking. Its divisions of space – sliding screens can partition the main living-room – are more precise, and the flow of inside and outside areas, on which Wright put so much emphasis, is missing.

Wright, for all his interest in Japanese houses, was not a designer for the frugal. He expected people to have cars, for example, and if his interiors are simple it is because his clients were doing so much outside. Many of the best modern small spaces have the fitted kitchens and walls of storage Wright was good at planning, but they have much to learn from the tighter arrangements which Rietveld created.

Gerrit Rietveld's famous Schroeder house (above) was built in 1924, with the very active participation of his client, Truus Schroeder, who is seen (above, left) standing behind the Rietveld Zig-Zag chairs. She lived the rest of her life here until her death in 1985. Space in the small house is maximized by sliding wall divisions on the upper floor and by a series of carefully interlocking spaces on the lower floor, which leave an open feel while defining areas for sitting, eating, sleeping and working. The house changed over the years, and so did Mrs Schroeder: age shortened her, and she needed a small stool (above, right) to reach cabinets custom-made for her in 1924. The two side panels of the ingenious mirror can be folded away.

ALMSHOUSES AND COLLEGES

This English almshouse (housing for old people), known as the New College of Cobham, in Kent, England, was established in 1598, and some of the building is even older. It originally contained twenty dwellings for the benefit of the parishes surrounding Cobham. Forty years ago bathrooms and lavatories were provided; this reduced the number to sixteen. Alterations in 1983 brought the number down to twelve, each with its own kitchen, bathroom, bedroom and living-room. The increase in the size of flats and the provision of small rooms rather than larger ones with dual functions (kitchen/living-room for example) is a reflection of rising standards and of user preference.

Student rooms and housing for old people are frequently built with public money, and therefore to what is regarded at any given time as reasonable minimum standards. Traditional forms – Oxford and Cambridge college buildings and old almshouses – have other things in common. Indeed, many almshouses are called colleges. Both are often built round a garden or lawn, and look like London squares of terrace or row houses. Both have entrance doors at regular intervals giving onto staircases, with living-rooms opening off them. Both may have communal buildings – chapels and

dining halls for example – attached.

Almshouse conversions have to bring old buildings up to the standard of new purpose-built flats. This almost invariably means making the accommodation more spacious, to meet public health standards.

The typical original almshouse unit had a very small living-room and a tiny bedroom, with lavatory and bathroom separate and shared. The new generation of old people entering the almshouse are used to higher standards of accommodation than their predecessors. The old view, that if people have enough to

'Ralph's digs in Cambridge', 1901 (far left) and a study-bedroom (left) in St Catherine's College, Oxford, designed by the Dane, Arne Jacobsen, in the 1960s. These rooms, like public housing, were built to official guidelines, which set limits on space. To the first working-class Oxbridge students the space they were allotted seemed princely, but things have changed. The two-room set has been replaced in new buildings by study-bedrooms with under-bed storage, built-in shelving and sofa-beds. On the other hand more bathrooms and more facilities for cooking are provided. Rooms imply functions: are you expected to give breakfast parties? To bath regularly? To have a boy- or girl-friend? Many students, not liking what the space says, follow Ralph and get out into digs.

eat and are warm and dry they will tolerate a shortage of space, is changing. The standards now applied are a modified version of the old Parker Morris standards for public housing, requiring approximately 450-500sq. ft (40-46sq. m) per person, including circulation space within the apartment but excluding public spaces.

One common way of converting an existing almshouse is to take two units and make a single four-roomed flat of them with kitchen, bathroom, bedroom and living-room. This is not as generous as it seems, for almshouses date back to before the time of universal old-age pensions, and couples now move into almshouses which in the past were filled with widows and widowers. This may be one reason why there is no move towards combining living

and sleeping spaces: as many small rooms as can be reasonably managed is the norm.

Students have seen a fall, not an increase, in provision. A pair of rooms – bedroom and living-room/study – was once the Oxford and Cambridge norm, as were college servants to make your bed, wash your coffee cups, and do the dusting. New student buildings (and conversions of old ones) rarely allow for more than a single space. St Catherine's College, Oxford, designed by Arne Jacobsen in the 1960s, is a good example of the norm, and its limitations. Jacobsen keeps the Oxbridge staircase principle, but the rooms themselves are single, and small – 10ft (3.05m) wide by 13 or 16ft (4 or 4.9m) deep.

The UK Universities Grants Committee, which sets the standards for new university buildings, did not

go as far as some. In Turkey there is a 169-page handbook called *Credits and Dormitories Law* which has a diagram showing the student how to lay out possessions in the closet. But try to fit a piano, a few paintings, an extensive wardrobe or a Brideshead-style breakfast party into this space: its limitations will become clear.

The other lesson of student rooms and old people's flats is that many people prefer clutter to order. In student rooms the neat shelving bulges with things other than books, posters spread from the pinboard provided to the wall (where the tape they are fixed with tears off the paint). Old people quite reasonably insist on having ornaments, framed photographs and large furniture.

No amount of planning can make up for lost space. It may be a luxury, but there is no substitute for the real thing.

MANHATTAN: A TWO-LEVEL CONVERSION

This elegant conversion of an East Side Manhattan apartment, in a building previously used as a seminary, is the work of New York architects Henry Smith-Miller and Laurie Hawkinson. Their design could be adapted to the conversion of the deep through-rooms typical of most London terrace houses and of New York Brownstones, which once dominated this part of Manhattan.

The personal needs — and even the physical characteristics — of their clients had a crucial influence on the architects' plans. Because the Marinos are both short people, the architects could take full advantage of the high ceiling to create a mezzanine level, a striking and unusual example of designing a space around the occupants' dimensions rather than some theoretical norm, and one which can maximize convenience in any small space.

Any satisfactory custom design must take the peculiar spatial demands of the intended occupants into account, whether they want to display an art collection, keep cats or work out in the bedroom. In this case, the design had to accommodate Dennis Marino's large book collection.

Book collecting can create serious problems in small spaces. The public library is the logical place to keep your novels, leaving only essential reference books such as dictionaries and telephone directories taking up shelf space at home. The architects' answer in this case was to create a substantial library on two storeys.

The two parts of the library can be cut off independently from the rest of the apartment by two versatile sets

The most dramatic feature of this Manhattan conversion (see also pages 51-52) is the centrally positioned staircase, visible from most parts of the apartment and dominating the exploded drawing on page 86. The winding or turning staircase is a classic formal device giving a sense of drama in large-scale architecture. Architects Henry Smith-Miller and Laurie Hawkinson prove it can work equally dramatically in a smaller space. The enclosed spiral staircase was a space-saving device in the medieval castle. This more open staircase gives an interesting contrast between curves and straight lines, with the rising curve leading up to a bedroom and the library adding to a feeling of height.

of floor-to-ceiling Japanese-style shoji screens (see page 52). These create privacy without sacrificing the possibility of large open spaces. The lower set of four screens divides the library from the eating area, while the matching set above cuts it off from an upper bedroom which is not permanently in use. Each set of screens can be put in any of nine positions. With the upper set closed and the lower set open, the bedroom and library become a spacious and private bed-sitting room.

Translucent glass replaces the traditional rice paper in the screens, reducing the risk of damage from flailing elbows, probing fingers and

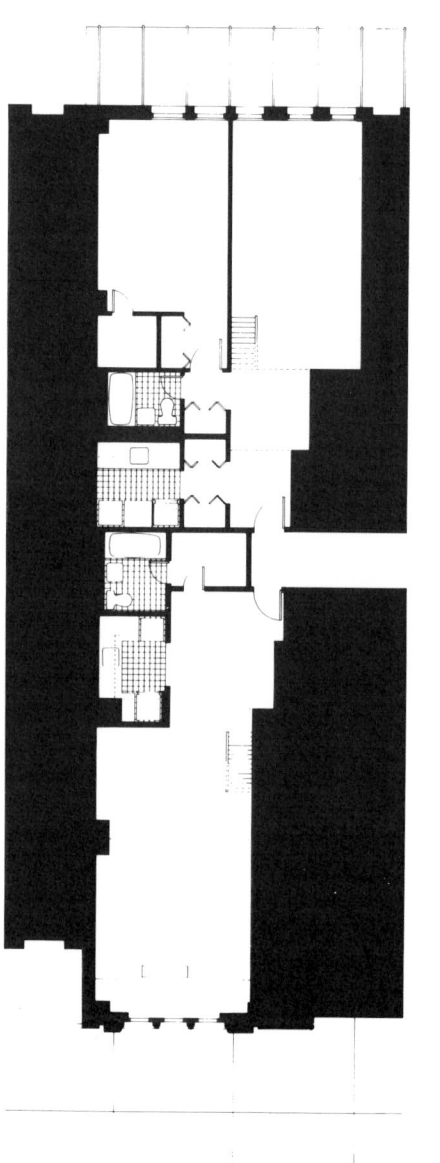

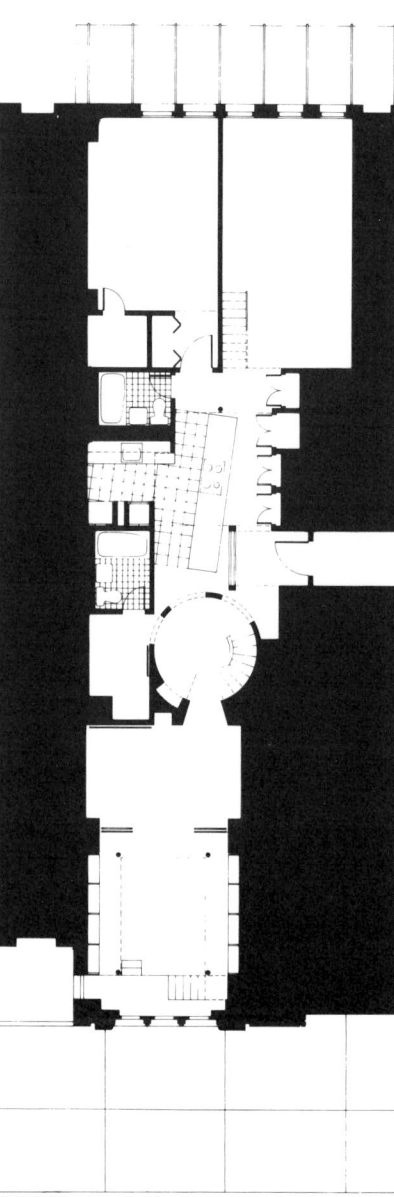

Facing: the kitchen and living areas of Eva Jiricna's small London flat, described on pages 89–90.

clawing cats. The brushed aluminium channels covering the sliding mechanism are a further departure from Japanese tradition. Aluminium poles are used to suspend the upper level from the ceiling.

The axonometric drawing of the flat (page 50) shows clearly the rotunda and the spiral staircase inside it leading to the mezzanine, where the Marinos' teenage daughter has her own room, potentially separate from the rest of the flat's activity. The staircase (page 85) is one of the most striking features of the flat. The wall enclosing the staircase is curved, creating the illusion of extra space around the corner, emphasizing the height of the apartment and making a central focus point.

A comparison of the 'before' and 'after' plans of the apartment on this pageshows where walls have been removed to enlarge the internal spaces. The design has opened up an uninterrupted view from front to back, recalling the old Brownstones and adding to the open feel of the flat.

The partial enclosure of spaces within the flat, as opposed to solid wall divisions, also contributes to the feeling of spaciousness. This is most clearly seen in the unusual positioning of the kitchen work island, which is set at an angle and juts out from the rest of the galley kitchen into the main through corridor.

Plans of the Marino apartment in New York, and of the two smaller apartments which were joined together to make it. The two existing bathrooms have been kept (do not change plumbing unless you have

to). The most dramatic changes have been made in the upper of the two original apartments – by extending the existing mezzanine and bringing stairs down from it to the room below.

Architect Eva Jiricna's small flat is one of the most inventive and stylish small spaces in London. When she moved into the elderly apartment block designed in the 1920s to house single people, the one-bedroom flat was in a desperately bad condition, and since she had spent every last penny on buying it, she had no money left for expensive modernization. The way she faced the challenge is an inspiration to anyone in similar circumstances. Her solutions are simple, inexpensive and easy to maintain.

How did she approach the design problem? Every flat, she believes, needs space for certain basic functions – sleeping, eating, sitting and watching television, cooking, washing and so on. If you assume these are the activities that will take place in the flat, you can look at the plan drawing and try to decide where each activity will take place.

Structural changes were minimal. She was not allowed to demolish any walls, but she changed the position of the door between the two main rooms (2 and 3 in the plan on page 90), moving it from the corner to create space for her bed (S in the plan) and the wall of storage with its mirrored doors. The new door now faces the other door in room 2,

creating a passageway through the flat.

Since she wanted to work at home, she designed a combined studio/bedroom (1 in the plan). The bed is a raised platform, with a frame of secondhand Dexion stove-enamelled black. Jiricna exploits Dexion framing in many of her projects. 'It's easy to cut, easy to spray, easy to assemble, it doesn't cost a fortune and it's easily changed if the function of the flat changes.'

The bed base and the doors of the cupboard alongside are perforated metal panels, folded over at the edges for strength and safety. The folding was done on a press by a local metalworking company. The same perforated metal is used for shelving in the flat, and for the space-saving table (O in the plan) which folds down from the wall when needed. The table swings down on a pair of pivots fixed to the wall and rests on a single pivoted leg which opens up and clicks into position. In the 'up' position, ball catches at each side of the table lock into sockets screwed to the wall.

Seating for the table is on a long bench which divides the sleeping and sitting area from the rest of the room, with additional seating provided by metal seat-height

occasional tables (N in the plan). The steps up to the studio/bedroom bed can also be used as seats.

The wooden bench across the living-room/spare bedroom is covered with green studded rubber flooring material, which is easy to cut to shape with a knife. The green flooring is used extensively in the flat – on the walls of the kitchen and bathroom for example.

White PVC flooring material covers the walls and ceiling in the spare bedroom, a typically novel and logical solution. 'I always think about easy maintenance,' she says, 'as I'm very busy. I thought that flooring would be durable – if people can walk on it, it should do the trick on the wall.' It hides the imperfections in a very blemished plaster wall surface. 'Replastering would have been expensive; it would have taken a long time to do it and a long time to dry before any wallpaper could be applied, and I hate decorating!'

The wall of storage is enclosed by floor-to-ceiling mirrored doors, which make the flat look bigger and reflect a lot of light from the window opposite. The house plants, which were losing leaves before the mirrors were installed, have responded well to the extra light.

The kitchen (page 87) in Eva Jiricna's London flat is tiny, as can be seen from the plan on page 90. Nevertheless, careful design allows her to cook satisfactorily for twenty people. Many features in the kitchen, as in the rest of the flat, were designed for non-domestic use. The shelves above the sink are cable trays supported on door stops; they hold plastic

bins for small-parts storage and face a useful set of shallow shelves. The easy-clean, green, studded-rubber wall covering was sold as flooring material. The same green rubber covers the barrier enclosing the versatile seating area. The seats can be used as single beds (the seat covers are duvets) or drawn together to form a double bed. The vertical blinds are

drawn across the room to give a guest privacy. The perforated metal table swings down from the wall when needed. Black industrial flooring covers the floor in both eating area and workroom/bed-room, seen from the metal bed platform in the photograph opposite. Despite the emphasis on space economy, she has found room for the essential easy chair.

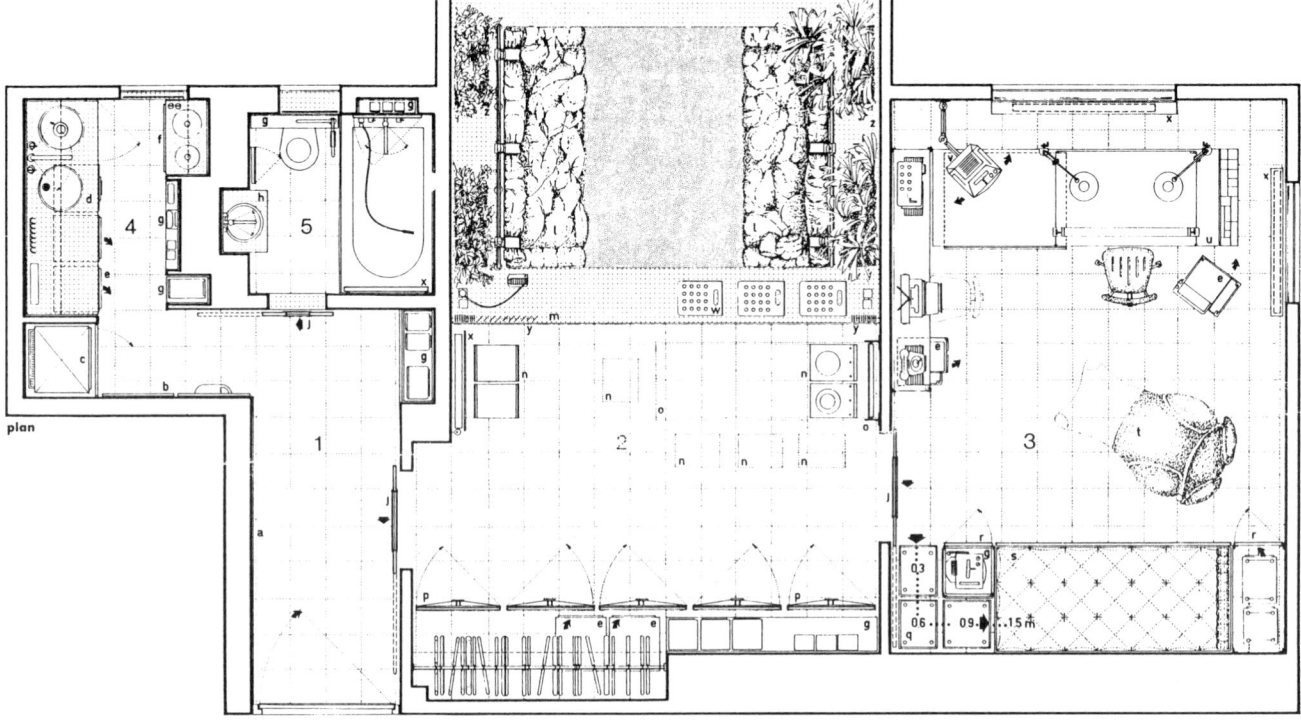

Eva Jiricna's plan of her small London apartment.

The storage space behind the mirror doors is fitted with shelving and hanging rails. Everything has its place. 'I know myself. I'm not a very tidy person. I knew that if everything didn't have its space I wouldn't put it away. I tried to use every square inch of space available.' She thinks it is wise to provide not only for what you own but for things you might acquire in the future.

Metal mesh on the walls provides extra storage; plants and lights hang from it in the spare bedroom. The lights, like other fittings, are from a boat chandler. 'I haven't got a boat, but it makes so much sense to use this equipment. It looks so good.'

Storage in the tiny, highly organized kitchen (4 in the plan) is on plastic-coated metal cable trays, which can span long distances without sagging, don't scratch, allow light to pass and need no maintenance. They rest on door stops screwed to the wall at each end. A set of space-saving shallow shelves covers one wall, deep enough for jars of coffee, tea, sugar, flour and similar items. A two-ring cooking hob is supplemented by a microwave oven set in the wall in the hall.

To save space throughout the flat, sliding doors are used, hung from standard sliding-door track. The sleeping/sitting area can be divided off for the privacy of overnight guests by drawing vertical louvers across it (Y in the plan). The two sofas – foam bases covered with carpet and duvets – can be used as single beds or drawn together to make a double bed.

Despite the originality and skill of her design, Eva Jiricna is encouraging about anyone's ability to create their own living space. 'Every person likes different materials and uses them differently. I think the only time that architects become human beings is when they have to design their own flats!' After all the client isn't paying for the work this time.

The flat is the first floor of a substantial terraced house in Kensington, London. The original plan is unchanged except for the removal of one partition wall. The largest room, at the front of the house, measures only 25 x 20ft (7.6 x 6.1m). It has a bay window and a French window which gives onto the roof of the front porch. This multi-functional room is used by its two owners as their work space, kitchen, drawing-room, dining-room and bedroom. The other rooms in the flat are two very small bedrooms, a narrow hall and a tiny bathroom which has enough room for a shower but not for a bath. The main room is heated by a single stove, the small bedrooms by bar fires. The small rooms can be heated up quickly when they are needed. Central heating is not necessarily the best way to heat a small space.

The owners are a couple in their fifties. He is a scholar, she a bookbinder, and both work at home. The tools of their trades are neatly stowed around desk and bench. Their three children have now left home. When they moved into the flat, their youngest daughter was fifteen and still living with them, and the flat was planned so that all three children could be accommodated if necessary.

The room is unusually high, allowing the construction of the functional bed platform which adds some 40sq. ft (3.7sq. m) to the floor area. The bed, on its raised platform, is reached by way of substantial steps which double as bookshelves (see photograph on page 34). A yacht-fitting on the side of the platform is particularly useful in preventing falls during descent.

The space below the platform is a closet of almost walk-in dimensions. Raising the head height by a few inches would have made it less awkward to use but would technically have created a habitable room, which would have been subject to all sorts of planning and building regulations. For planning purposes, the owners sleep on top of the wardrobe, which is acceptable to the authorities.

The kitchen mirrors the bed platform. It is divided from the rest of the room by a counter top which has storage space above and below. The fridge is on the counter side, with the cooker and sink fixed along the back wall. An oval dining table stands free in the main room. The absence of sharp corners makes it less obtrusive and less bruising than a rectangular table, and the oval is more economical of space than a circle.

The first impression is one of ordered profusion. The space is tidy, rather than tidied up, but far from minimal. The owners have a lot of ornaments on display, although nearly all the paintings are small. Wall space is limited by one-room living, especially where, as here, there is a large number of books to be shelved (see pages 33-34). The side of the book shelf behind the desk and in front of the bed is used to suspend scissors, adhesive tape and other small office items. The sides of other shelves are covered with a lattice of tapes, so the vertical surface can be put to use as a notice board, another way of storing papers. This is just one among many examples of commonly ignored small surfaces being used in the flat. Storage is extremely organized – it has to be in such a crowded small space. 'Everyone must know where everything is,' according to their daughter.

Many activities take place in the one room but, as one of the owners commented, 'one does not eat, sleep, write books, bind books, cook, sit and talk all at once!' Nevertheless, communal living on this kind of scale requires, in the words of their daughter, 'structuring your tolerance', by which she means anticipating when others will be home and preparing for the expected arrival. Disruptions to regular routine – the arrival of illness or visitors for example – cause problems. If a sick person is occupying the room twenty-four hours a day, the other normal activities must often be suspended. It is wise to plan for such eventualities if possible. The owners say the big room would not work so well if there were not the smaller rooms.

Although they live in this flat most of the time, the owners also have a cottage where they spend summer weekends. There is no doubt that having another place to keep large things, such as mammoth pieces of inherited furniture, makes small-space living less rigorous. A very important feature of the London flat is that all three people have their own private space for dressing and keeping their clothes. It is also the case that this kind of living is more suitable to people who are

LONDON: ONE-ROOM LIVING AND WORKING

The steps up to the bed structure (left) in the working/living-room provide much-needed extra book storage. Storage-in-stairs is a useful and widely used space-saver (see other examples on page 121). The space under the bed has been converted into a large enclosed storage area, which disguises the bed as you enter the room.

'continuously interested in the environment', as their daughter tactfully put it.

The most interesting feature of the flat is that it was not designed by an architect but planned by its owners. With small interiors this is obviously a great advantage. The under-stair shelving was custom made for a specific set of albums. The height of closets and the width of working spaces in the kitchen were worked out by reaching up to see where the shelves would be convenient for the users, and walking with a full glass in either hand to see how much space was needed for two people to pass each other in safety.

The detailing of all the woodwork is neat, an important consideration in compact spaces where everything is close to the eye of the beholder. Most of the joinery is varnished or stained pine and plywood. It is the kind of work a good amateur carpenter could manage, particularly as no structural changes have been made. Although a considerable quantity of timber was employed, which nowadays would be costly, the outlay in money and time would have been far greater in a larger flat. The small space does after all have real advantages over the palace.

LONDON: COLOUR AND IMAGINATION

By the inventive use of colour Simon Withers and Christos Tolera effected a dramatic, inexpensive transformation for a client who had moved into a sleazy rental apartment over an Italian pizza house in a Victorian building in Soho, London. Their work provides an object lesson in exploiting the features of an existing interior, however unpromising.

The apartment (see also photographs on page 69) was deeply dirty when they arrived. It took six weeks and the removal of four truckloads of rubbish before work could begin on its two rooms and small bathroom. Six layers of greasy, crumbling carpet were lifted, revealing newspapers dating from 1946. Not an encouraging start, and matters deteriorated when walls fell down and ceilings collapsed.

Nevertheless, the two undaunted decorators carried on with the hard work of stripping down all the surfaces themselves. They believe this is an important stage, which helps them develop a feeling for the space and its possibilities, a real pay-off of doing the work yourself.

Withers also suggests that painting your entire interior white is a wise move before you begin using colours, allowing you time to think about what you want.

They provided their client with a couple of watercolour drawings to show what they were trying to achieve, but everything changed as work proceeded and the unsavoury realities of the structure emerged from the dust.

The doorcase into the front room bore the scars of a recent clumsy

Furnishing in the London flat (above) is minimal: a curious bone chair and table stand alone. The damaged woodwork has been spattered with paint for a granite-like finish.

break-in, and when the paint was removed it became clear that a fresh application of paint would be needed to hide the burns and blemishes. Rather than replacing the damaged part of the frame where the lock had been knocked off, they simply hollowed out the scar and painted the frame to look like stone. The damaged section now looks like a dramatic chip in expensive stonework. The same stone effect is carried around the baseboards and window frames in the room. The principle of honesty to materials makes little sense when the materials are so poor and the budget so low.

The main feature in the living-room is a mural reminiscent of the statues on Easter Island, painted by special request of the client. It has some fifteen layers of paint—a stabilizer to hold the wall together, three undercoats and three coats of the terracotta base colour went on before drawing began. This was varnished and softened with chalk dust. Then parts of the wall were covered in masking tape and six coats of paint added before the tape was removed to create the torn-paper effect. The work was time-consuming but inexpensive, since the areas of paintwork in the apartment are not large.

The mural covers the apartment's only stable wall. When they removed the paper from the partition wall separating the two main rooms, part of the wall collapsed.

They took full advantage of the calamity by removing the damaged sections of plaster between the wooden studs in the wall framework and fitting purpose-built boxes to the shapes that emerged. The boxes, which are constructed from 1in (25mm) pine, protrude about 2in (50mm) into the room at each side; they provide storage space and bring light through from the front windows to the otherwise gloomy room at the back of the house.

The smaller room has become the bedroom – all rooms were bedrooms in the apartment's recent colourful past. The original panelling in the wall appeared only as soft-edged bulges under acres of paper. Paper and paint were stripped off and the panels relined.

Each panel was treated in the same way. They wanted to create an effect of ageing on the wall – a wise decision since signs of ageing are everywhere. They began by painting on three coats of white undercoat. Having decided that the panels would receive most wear in the centre, where people would rub against the wall, they painted a thick single coat of translucent yellow all around the edge of each panel and worked it in slowly towards the centre with a dry brush, leaving a

white highlight in the centre.

This technique is simple to master, demanding very little paint and very little expense, but a large outlay of care and patience. Similar principles are involved in the treatment of the panel frame and door in the small room. The removal of the thick paint from door and frame left them chipped and burned. The decorators decided against the obvious solution – replacement. Nor did they bother to fill in any holes. They used black oil paint applied around the edges and brushed out towards the centre with a dry brush, as on the panels. In this way they picked out details on the wood and touched in more signs of age.

The tiny bathroom is a bizarre mixture of the exotic and the ordinary. A white wc, a plain white hand-basin on a pedestal and a simple unpanelled white cast-iron bathtub with traditional chromium-plated taps stand inside a sort of marine grotto.

Replastering became necessary in the bathroom when the ceiling collapsed on the builders. Withers and Tolera thought plain plaster or wallpaper would be too boring, so they cut extensive cracks into the new plaster with a knife, applied pigments in the cracks and wiped off the excess from the plaster surface before the pigment dried.

The heavily textured surface which rises from the floor to dado height is concrete, pressed by a gloved hand over a chicken-wire framework and ground to shape. It is covered in molten carnauba wax burned into the surface with a heater, an old technique Withers

discovered during library research into the art of the eighteenth-century decorators.

Two additional features complete the marine feel of the bathroom. The baseboard along the back wall has been brought forward several inches and the space behind it filled with a trough of sand which absorbs some of the moisture from the damp room. Sponges have been pressed around the window frame where they look alarmingly like a serious invasion by dry rot.

Perhaps the most remarkable feature of the apartment is the complete absence of a kitchen. A coffee machine and a small fridge are the only signs of domesticity. The occupant claims no competence as a cook and did not want cooking smells invading his small space. Since restaurants are open at any hour in the surrounding streets of Soho, he has no need to cook for himself. This is an admirable space-saver for city-centre living if you can afford to eat out.

The furnishings are minimal. A table and chair, an easy chair and a brass bed stand on bare floorboards. The windows are covered by unobtrusive narrow-slatted Venetian blinds. All the drama is in the decoration.

Neither Withers nor Tolera has any formal training, and they are encouraging about anyone's ability to achieve equally stunning low-cost effects in their own small rooms. 'It's a matter of not being worried,' says Withers. 'You can always change it. If a colour goes wrong or you decide you don't like it you can just put another on top.'

Plans, diagram and section show the intricate structure and planning of Ferrari's work on the Milan apartment. The staircase follows the obtuse angle of the wall and leads up to the bedspace. This is surrounded by cupboards at ceiling level: below them is an opening giving a view down into the main room. The kitchen wraps round two sides of the bathroom, which gets light through the glass blocks of which the wall above sink height is constructed.

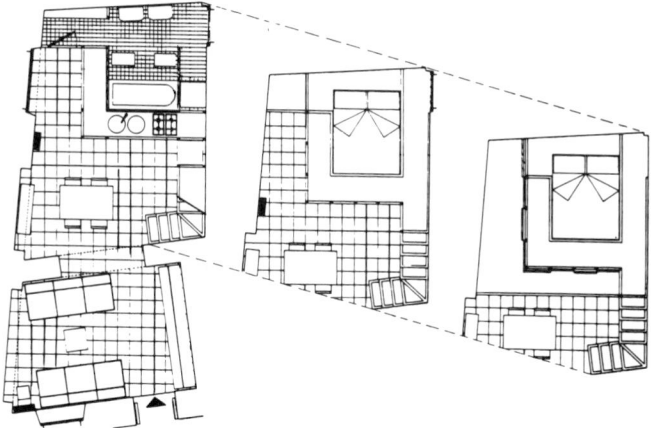

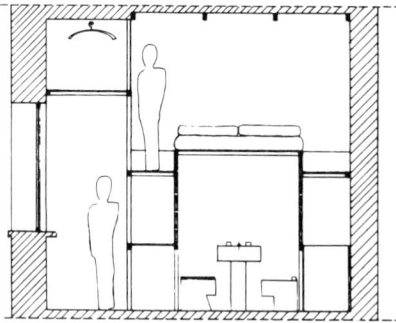

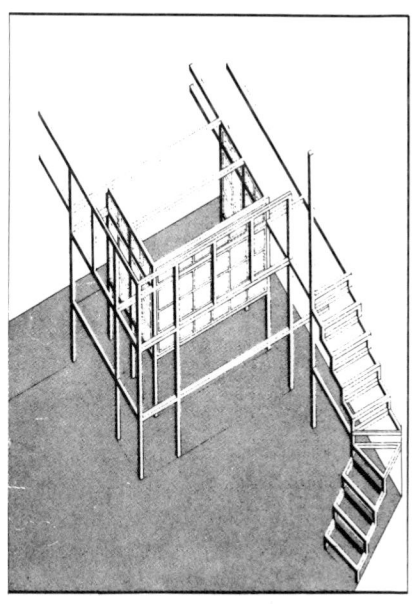

Architect Alessandro Ferrari's conversion of a tiny, awkwardly shaped city-centre apartment in a fifteenth-century building in a Milan courtyard is an inspiration for anyone trying to pack all the necessary functions of an apartment into an extremely compact space. The meticulous planning of an ingenious and elegant custom-designed platform construction (see also photograph on page 70) has made it possible to fit a fully operational kitchen, bathroom and bedroom into less than one quarter of the apartment's total floor area of 430sq. ft (40sq. m).

The extent to which the architect has respected surviving elements in the ancient structure, in spite of the pressures on space, is remarkable. The old brick arches which emerged when layers of plaster were removed remains as an important decorative feature, defining areas within the apartment. A massive timber beam has also been left exposed.

The entrance door opens directly from the courtyard into the fairly conventional living-room, where there are two low-level bed/settees facing each other over a low coffee table. Keeping the furnishings low is a standard way of increasing the sense of space within a room. The only tall piece of furniture in the room is the glass-fronted bookcase against the wall.

Careful decoration unifies the spaces within the apartment. The 12 x 12in (300 x 300mm) grey terracotta tile flooring in the living-room is taken through into the dining area which opens up under the old brick arch. The old wood dining table is covered in a sheet of yellow vinyl matching the cladding on the stair treads leading up to the platform, which is the most remarkable feature of the apartment.

The platform contains kitchen, bathroom and, above them, the bedroom with its surprisingly extensive storage which does not impair the feeling of openness in the platform block.

The twin keys to the success of the platform are its open construction and the meticulous measurement of the spaces within it. The section drawing shows how carefully human dimensions were not only taken into account but exploited to maximize use of space. The area occupied by the bed is raised to a higher level than the surrounding walkway. This allows adequate headroom in the bathroom directly below the bed. The sunken walkway gives easy access to the eye-level closets, with their space-saving sliding doors, which surround the bedroom without enclosing it.

Ferrari has happily avoided the temptation to provide access to the platform via a ladder. The staircase, which makes for a much more comfortable climb up to bed, is not a waste of space, since the large fridge and gas boiler are neatly fitted under it. A shelf built into the stairs adds to storage in the apartment and obscures the vent from the boiler.

The open staircase is an integral part of the platform structure, and is built of the same materials finished in the same way. The structural elements in both the platform and the stairs leading up to it are unclad, so that the space they contain is not closed off from the rest of the apartment. For structural stability, the open-plan construction had to be

The television is packed away among the wire trays in the closets running around the upper half of the platform (right). The lines of the radiator blend with those of the platform structure. The glass-block wall which lets light into the bathroom is reflected (far right) in the room's large mirrors, which also increase the feeling of space.

built of strong materials. Ferrari chose square-section iron $2\frac{3}{8}$ x $2\frac{3}{8}$ in (60 x 60mm), painted grey.

The kitchen is built around the edge of the platform structure. This, too, is very open. The stainless steel worktop, double sink, four-burner unit and dishwasher are not enclosed. The cooker hood, which is necessary to prevent cooking smells polluting the small apartment, is transparent and therefore unobtrusive.

The splashback in the kitchen is also the wall of the new bathroom,

directly under the bed. Three of the bathroom walls are glass blocks, much loved by architects of the modern movement and used to stunning effect in the Maison de Verre in Paris, whose translucent glass blocks form the entire front wall of the house. Built by Pierre Chareau between 1928 and 1931, the Maison de Verre is perhaps the first true high-tech building, and it is crammed with ideas for small-space designers. The effect of the glass blocks is well suited to small spaces, letting in a soft diffused light

giving the impression of open spaces beyond while providing a significant degree of privacy.

The illusion of space is enhanced in the Ferrari bathroom by the use of mirrors along the tiled fourth wall, reflecting the glass blocks. Ferrari has chosen substantial bevel-edged mirrors in preference to the more usual mirror tiles, a degree of attention to detail which is apparent throughout this apartment, whose lessons will be welcomed by small-space livers well beyond the confines of its old courtyard in Milan.

KITCHENS

Keen cooks in small spaces can take enouragement from the fact that many good cooks prefer a tiny kitchen, where everything is within easy reach. The post-war trend is towards minimal kitchens, typified by the influential 1949 kitchen which American architect Philip Johnson built in his Glass House in New Canaan, Connecticut, with its below-counter appliances.

In a city building divided into apartments you are likely to find the kitchen crammed into a converted closet. Small kitchens make good sense in big cities, where people tend to eat out a lot. However, a rival movement is gaining ground, with the trend towards the large farmhouse-style kitchen, in which most household activities can take place.

If you always eat out, you may need no more than a coffee machine and a minuscule fridge, backed up perhaps by a toaster-oven and a few emergency snacks. Ethel Merman is the inspiration for this bold approach. She had the kitchen torn out of her Park Lane and Berkshire Hotel apartments, and relied totally on a toaster-oven which she used for reheating food – room service supplied all the rest. The take-out restaurant will take the place of room service, four-burner cooker, freezer, storage cabinets and work counters for today's city dweller.

Modern food developments can help extremists save space, even though the food pill popular in 1950s science fiction must be abandoned in the name of a high-fibre diet. The food on the science-fact space shuttle is developed from

Small kitchens can prepare big meals. A crew of seventy is fed from this cramped kitchen on a British submarine.

military survival rations and camping supplies, and manufactured by the names in almost every fridge – Coca Cola, Carnation, Green Giant, Kelloggs and General Mills.

The vacuum-packed gourmet meal has become a standard item in some surprisingly prestigious restaurant kitchens, and can limit the need for complex cooking appliances – and washing-up – at home. The boil-in-the-bag kipper is particularly desirable in a small space as it keeps unpleasant smells down. Frying food generates smells, and since it is extremely easy to buy fried food ready-cooked, it can be banned from the small kitchen. If you decide to cook at home, you start eating space. Experts calculate that you need some 3sq. ft (0.25sq. m) even to chop an onion in comfort.

The kitchen can be the most expensive room in the house to refit. Americans spent some $7 billion on kitchen renovations in 1985, almost double the bathroom bill. Careful planning saves money.

A kitchen should ideally face

north-east or north-west, but economics dictate that the kitchen should be installed near existing gas and electricity supplies, hot- and cold-water supply pipes and the outside soil stack, where the sink water will drain along with the waste water from bath/shower, wc, hand basin, dishwasher and washing-machine. Pipes from the sink can easily be run under floorboards – but not so easily under concrete – for short distances. The sink should not be over 7ft 6in (2.3m) from the waste stack.

There are other considerations to take into account in your kitchen design. Do you want space for eating in the kitchen? If not, the kitchen should be convenient for the eating area. Do you want space for washing clothes? Do you want to watch television while you are cooking? Will you be able to extract cooking smells, through an outside wall for example? Where are you going to store awkward items such as step-ladders and brooms?

A good view may be important if you spend a lot of time in the kitchen, but for safety reasons, cookers should not be in front of a window or in line of draughts through doors, nor should the burners or sink be at the open end of a run of units. Units fixed over the burners are also unsafe.

Facing rows of appliances should ideally be no closer than 4ft (1.2m). For easy access to a low-level cooker, allow a similar space in front of it. Applying these principles in tiny kitchens can call for great ingenuity. Custom-built cabinets and dual-purpose units can help.

Much work has been done on the space a normal human being needs to carry out standard kitchen tasks. These studies have influenced the design of kitchen fittings and equipment, and their conclusions are worth considering when you design your own kitchen, although custom design – which can maximize the use of a small space – means you can make the kitchen right for you.

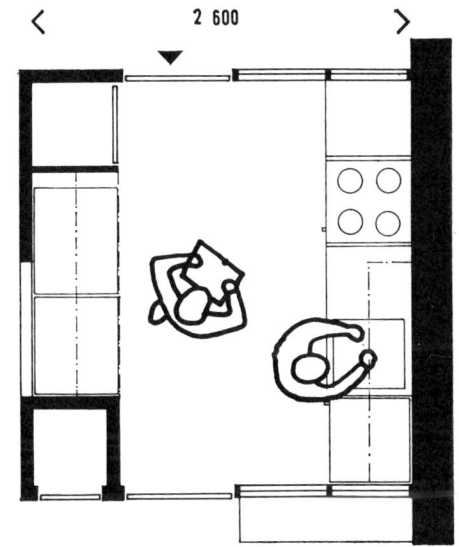

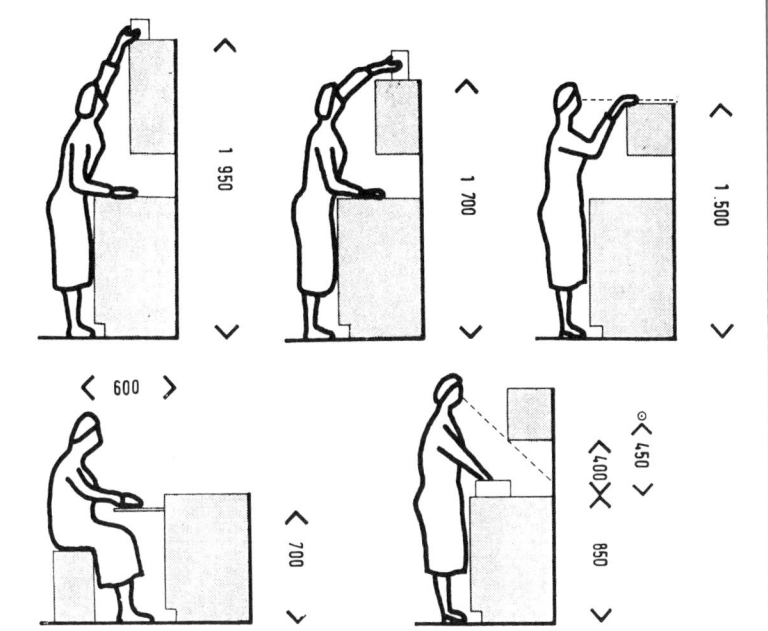

The drawings on this page are taken from Space in the Home by the UK Department of the Environment. The drawings assume a woman 5ft 4in (1630mm) tall is using the kitchen. They show the maximum vertical reach over a work counter (top, left), the maximum comfortable reach (top, centre) and a shelf at eye level (top, right). The drawings above show how work counters and wall-mounted cabinets will influence sightlines (right), and a comfortable seat-height for working (left). A range of current kitchen equipment, giving maximum, average and minimum dimensions, is shown below. All measurements are in millimetres.

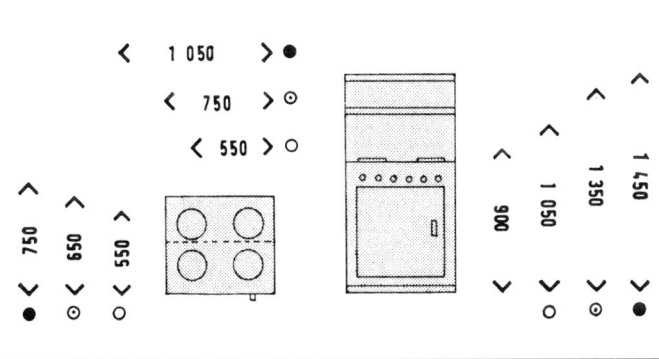

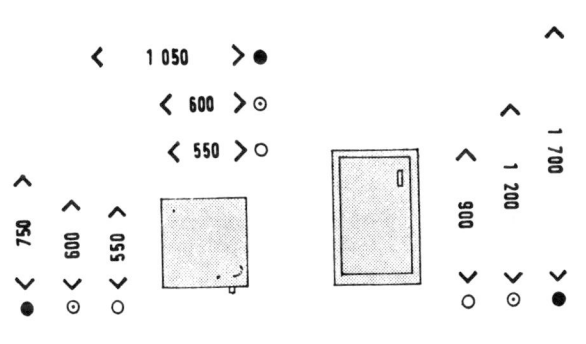

We may all have to wash up, but we do not have to put it all away. A plate-drying rack can also serve as a storage cabinet and display shelf, saving space and time in any kitchen. Ready-made racks can be bought in kitchen supply shops, but they will not necessarily use a restricted or awkwardly shaped space to full advantage. Incorporating a do-it-yourself rack is a sensible and simple project if you are designing a small kitchen.

Dowel plate racks come in many forms. They can be made with open ends or solid sides. The crockery can be supported by a single row of vertical dowels at the back or by two parallel rows at front and back. They can be fitted with an additional row of short projecting dowels for

glasses, while hooks can be screwed to the underside to hold mugs and cups. They can be several storeys high. The rack can be fixed overhead, either against the wall or suspended from the ceiling on metal rods fixed to the ceiling joists. Choose a design you like, which suits your purpose and is the right height for the person washing up.

The length of the rack will depend on the space available and on the amount of crockery you want to store. It is wise not to extend the plate rack beyond the limits of the draining board below, to prevent water dripping where it is unwanted. Shelves could be fitted to the wall above the rack and the entire unit hidden behind sliding glass doors to create a cupboard.

In both the neo-baronial granite-walled basement kitchen of Edwin Lutyens's Castle Drogo (above right), and within the storage area which surrounds the sink in the Post Modernist kitchen in Charles Jencks's London house (below), dishes are stored in draining racks. Kitchens – the only rooms in houses where manual work is regularly done – are the rooms where ergonomic studies make best sense. The draining rack (particularly if combined with a double sink) does away with much drying of dishes, and much walking from cupboard to sink. In a small kitchen it saves space, because it acts both as drainer and storage. The reach of the shortest regular dishwasher determines the height of the top rack, the number of dishes the length. Racks are usually unpainted, and made of standard dowel rods in a wooden frame. Fully loaded, the rack is heavy: fixing it to the wall, and seeing that the frame is well braced, are the principal design constraints.

A rack with solid sides connected by a pair of horizontal dowels at top and bottom is perhaps the simplest to make. To simplify construction the four horizontal dowels should be larger in diameter than the verticals between which the crockery is slotted. The four could, if you prefer, be square-section timber, which could make it easier to fix hooks for additional drainage and storage capacity.

If you fit two rows of vertical dowels, they must obviously be parallel. To mark the points where holes should be drilled, hold all four dowels to your workbench, making sure they are square, and draw lines across all four where the sockets will be. Drill holes half way through the dowels. Holes are drilled half way through the inside face of the side panels to take the four horizontals. The unit can then be assembled dry to check that it all fits before it is glued together using a waterproof woodworking adhesive.

Classic kitchen design is based on the work triangle, defined by the three key appliances involved in the cooking sequence – the fridge, the cooker and the sink. The perfect arrangement is widely believed to be a line leading from work counter to cooker to counter to sink to counter, with the line unbroken by doorways, passageways or full-height appliances such as an eye-level oven or tall industrial refrigerator. The sink should be no more than 6ft (1.8m) from the cooker, rarely a problem in a small space.

The choice of basic kitchen layouts is limited. Simplest is the galley kitchen, inspired by seagoing

Where there is no room for a separate kitchen in a small apartment, the hideaway kitchen may be the answer. The space-saving kitchen unit (below) includes a two-burner stove, fridge, sink, water heater and storage. After use it can be shut away (top photograph) behind the closet doors, which are exploited to give extra storage space on the fridge-door principle. Mounting the garbage can on the door makes it desirably accessible. Flooring must be chosen with care, since it must work and look right both in a kitchen and a dining/sitting area. Cork, vinyl or ceramic tiles are possible solutions. Smells can also be a problem – a vent to the outside air would improve the environment. Make sure door-hung cloths will not touch hot burners when the doors close.

kitchens, in which all the appliances and work counters are in a single line. This type can be fitted in a corridor. Given a space at least 6ft (1.8m) wide, you can fit a double galley, with a row of appliances along one wall facing a row of shallow shelves. It is important to make sure the fridge and cupboard doors are hinged on the more convenient side and that you have somewhere to put hot dishes down.

This is a problem in the tiny kitchen preparing the food for the seventy-strong crew in a Royal Navy 'O' class submarine, where the cooks complain that the lack of space doesn't allow them to keep food once it is cooked in the kitchen's two ovens. The confined space also means the cook must work alone – there is no room for an assistant. The lack of ventilation which forces up the temperature and creates a lot of steam is a further common complaint. Kitchen ventilation helps fight condensation and improves comfort.

The food in the submarine is cooked in square pans, which maximize use of space on the burners. A front rail stops the pans falling off the range when the boat lurches, and could be useful at home where small children are jumping around the kitchen. Unfortunately it cannot prevent the contents slopping out in rough seas. The system would work better in a land-based kitchen.

Two rows of appliances face each other in the submarine kitchen. The entrance door closes to become a serving hatch and to create a U-shaped kitchen, which is a good user of available kitchen space. A simple

Rolling storage units like the one on the left can make better use of narrow, deep spaces than standard shelves, cabinets or drawers. Access from both sides effectively creates a pair of shallow shelves rather than one deep one.

Small fridges like the Minicool (below) measure only about 2ft high and 18in wide and deep (610 x 480 x 480mm). Although sold mainly for use in hotel rooms and caravans, they can be useful in small kitchens at home.

Small cookers (below) can provide oven, two rings, and grill in a space only 12 x 12 x 6in (300 x 300 x 150mm). Many miniature cookers can be plugged directly into a standard socket outlet, which often means a big saving on the installation costs of special wiring.

galley can also be converted into an L-shaped kitchen, with counters and appliances along adjoining walls, though the space where they meet in the corner can be difficult to use. Tall appliances should be fitted at the end of the run to avoid breaking into the work counters.

A peninsular kitchen can be used to separate the kitchen from other areas while allowing communication between the two. The projecting peninsula can be used as a serving area as well as a work counter or breakfast bar.

Adequate storage is essential. American kitchen storage standards are useful guidelines even if your space is too small to meet them. Minimum shelf area for storage is 30sq. ft (2.79sq. m), and minimum

drawer area 6sq. ft (0.56sq. m). The inaccessible space inside a corner cupboard counts as only 50 per cent of its shelf area, while a corner carousel unit counts as its actual shelf area. At least a third of the shelf area should be in a cupboard, and 60 per cent or more should be behind cupboard doors. In a small space, cupboard doors may feel less oppressive if they are made of glass. Glass is, of course, waterproof, and glass mirrors make a practical, space-creating splashback.

To begin planning storage, list all the items to be stored in the kitchen, including easily forgotten items such as ironing-boards, brooms, fresh food, kettle, toaster and cookbooks. Shelves are inexpensive and simple to fit. They allow you to exploit

awkward spaces in alcoves, inside walls, behind doors and in front of windows. Shallow shelves – the depth of a single can or jar – are convenient space-savers, leaving everything on the shelf in view and reachable without calamities. They are perfect for jars of dried or canned food, bottles and spices.

These items can also be stored on shelves fitted on the inside face of a door, a solution used extensively by refrigerator manufacturers. Indeed, a fridge-door storage compartment from an obsolete appliance can be unscrewed and remounted inside a kitchen cupboard.

Cabinets are the basic storage unit. Access to the space inside can be improved if the entire cabinet slides out. This can also provide an

The US-made King mini-kitchen – a basic, inexpensive, factory-assembled compact kitchen, with sink, stove and fridge (with a small freezer) in one unit. A lid comes down to make the kitchen unobtrusive. Optional extras include overhead microwave oven, wall cabinets, waste disposers, range hoods and light fixtures. The smallest measures only 30in (760mm) wide, 36in (910mm) high and 24in (610mm) deep.

The Baby Belling (below): the original small electric stove, designed for use in submarines and standard equipment in the British bed-sitting-room for decades.

The fully transportable German-made Kitcase (below) allows you to change your mind about the position of the kitchen. You simply join its pressure hose to the water supply, its drain pipe to the drains, plug it into an ordinary socket and turn on the power, and you have a working kitchen on wheels with two burners, freezer, fridge, coffee machine, electric water heater and sink.

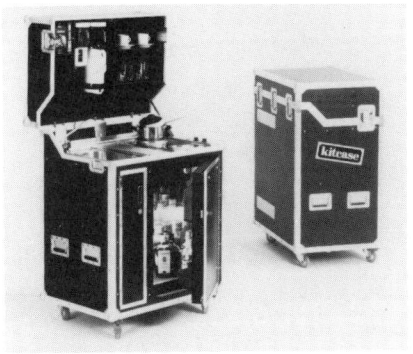

extra low-level work counter, for the preparation of pastry, for example.

Wire baskets fitted inside a rolling cupboard will stop things tumbling out when the trolley is on the move. Wire baskets are particularly suitable for fresh food storage, as they allow air to circulate.

Wire mesh has other uses. Kitchen gadgets can be hung from hooks on a mesh mounted on the wall. Such objects can be decorative, although a display of unsheathed knives is a little dangerous. A sharp knife is the most basic piece of kitchen equipment. Other indispensables could include a sharpener for the knife, a can-opener, bottle-opener, potato-peeler, grater, ladle, sieve, scissors,

whisk, spatula, measuring-jug, strainer, timer, the versatile Chinese cleaver and finally the wooden spoon. You may also want to display the menu from the local take-out restaurant rather prominently.

Beware of gadgetry. Manufacturers of kitchen appliances have consistently reduced the versatility of utensils. Many can now perform only one specialized task – cooking only hot dogs or only pancakes for example. These are a waste of space in small kitchens, unless you exist on hot dogs and pancakes.

The great all-purpose kitchen gadget was the servant, although people complained constantly about them not working properly. Servants made Georgian houses such flexible

spaces. Servants running around the house carrying things to where they were needed meant no fixed services were necessary.

Maximizing work surfaces is the art of good kitchen design. The perfect counter is easy to clean and durable enough to withstand both hot pans and sharp knives. Unfortunately, most easy-clean surfaces look vile when they are dirty. Plastic laminates are easily scorched by hot pans and scarred by chopping meat and vegetables. Improve the versatility of your counters with a wooden chopping block and pastry board which pull out of a cupboard like a drawer or fit over the sink.

The small space is a danger to your body and your mind, and

nowhere is more dangerous than the kitchen. The kitchen is the domestic murderer's favourite spot; the weapons come readily to hand. On the whole, wives kill husbands in kitchens, husbands kill wives in bedrooms.

SMALL EQUIPMENT

Modern technology has simplified the design of small kitchens. The microwave oven is an obvious space saver, as long as you do not use it only as a very expensive kettle for boiling water. The waste-disposal unit is a great temptation where space is limited.

The small kitchen is a place for custom design, but standard units should be used where possible, as they are much cheaper than most custom-made alternatives. Most appliances and cabinets are sold in standard sizes. The standardization of cabinet sizes began in America after the Second World War, and this in turn influenced the size of the appliances which fit in and around them.

Many American-built appliances and cabinets are larger than European equivalents. Today's standard US work counter is 36in (910mm) high and 24in (610mm) deep, the same depth as both standard dishwashers and stoves. In Europe, base unit height is 35in (900mm), with a standard depth of 600mm, half an inch shallower than the American model. It is of course relatively easy to saw off the back section of an overdeep unit. The backs are often flimsy and can be removed and refitted without difficulty. Twenty inches (500mm)

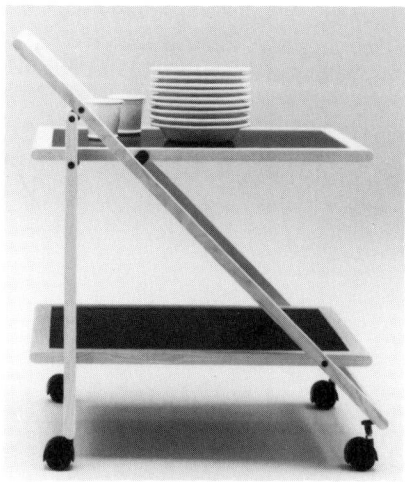

A trolley is a simple solution to the need for a little more working surface in more than one place. This one can be folded when not in use.

can be considered a practical minimum depth.

Many extremely useful custom fittings are designed to fit in the standard units. Such items as corner carousels can significantly improve the convenience of cabinets.

The perfect height for cabinets and work counters will depend on the cook's dimensions. Custom design can guarantee satisfaction. Whether you choose standard or custom-made items, it is wise to keep the height and size of all units uniform to avoid visual confusion. For the same reason, a uniform colour can improve the looks of a small kitchen. Even the fridge can be painted or spray-enamelled to match the rest of the kitchen.

Manufacturers on both sides of the Atlantic are now producing kitchen units and appliances smaller than the established standard sizes, making it possible to pack more equipment into the tiniest kitchen. Refrigerators, dishwashers, cookers, microwave ovens and washing-machines are all shrinking. Italian dishwashers, for example, will fit under a standard work counter and can be rolled out on telescopic runners to fill them with four full place settings.

Small equipment has always been made for boats and caravans, where space is usually tight. Boat and caravan shows can be worth a visit even if you never intend to take a mobile vacation.

Most people find life without a refrigerator too tough. Fridges designed for hotel bedrooms, offices and caravans may be useful in a small kitchen. If you don't shop often, a large-capacity fridge becomes vital. Standard capacity is 13cu. ft (370 litres), but models taking only half that can be found. Small fridges can be used free standing, built into a ventilated cabinet or wall-mounted on brackets. Doors can be hinged left or right for convenience.

Absorption-type fridges are quieter than the normal compressor system, which is an advantage in a small kitchen.

The choice of compact and modular kitchens—all combining small versions of standard kitchen appliances in a single unit—is growing greater, as their dimensions grow smaller. In a space 30in (760mm) wide you can have an oven, burners, refrigerator, sink and storage. Optional variations include built-in lighting, garbage disposal units and coffee makers.

BATHROOMS

Sit-up tubs take up less floor space than conventional ones, and if your bath has a view they have other advantages. This range takes picture-window bathing to an extreme. They are to be found in a cable car in Wakayama Prefecture, Japan, which takes the happy bathers out over the sea. The Japanese take their bathing very seriously, considering a soak in almost unbearably hot water to be one of life's major pleasures, not merely a convenient way of keeping clean. There is no need to sacrifice the luxury of a hot bath in the interests of saving space. Small Japanese baths are becoming increasingly available in the West, and take up little more floorspace than a standard shower.

Although the baths of ancient Rome are famous, the bathroom is still by no means a universal fitting in the European home. Obsessive space savers might decide to continue the no-bathroom tradition and use the bathing facilities in public baths, swimming pools and gymnasiums. Others will have no choice.

The need to save space and to minimize water consumption in submarines rules out the provision of baths and encourages the submariners' tendency to avoid washing both body and clothes. Most people would find the cramped submarine shower, washroom and

wc frankly uninviting, with dials, pipes and gauges everywhere. The sturdy equipment does have a certain high-tech appeal. Both hand-basin and wc are made of stainless steel. A stainless steel splashback also covers the raised back lip of the basin – a neat protection against splashes. The mirrors over the basins, with their anchor motif, are edged in black rubber and supported by clips at top and bottom.

Fitting bathrooms into minimal spaces is not in itself a new development. In nineteenth-century Scottish tenements, for instance, the hand basin would be set over the

bath to save space. This curious arrangement no longer appears among the many plans for small bathrooms illustrated in manuals serving the architectural profession and readily available in bookshops and libraries.

Most space-saving plans rely on full exploitation of the floor area unoccupied by fittings. For example, a person beside the bath will be standing in the same space as when using the hand basin or wc. Such multiple use of space is sensible, though the most economical layout from the financial point of view is to place all the appliances against one wall.

Work has been done on the amount of space the average human being needs to go through the average bathroom routines, from leaning over the wash basin to towelling your back after a bath. The results of all this research are published in books such as the UK Department of the Environment's *Space in the Home*. Here you will learn that you need 43 x 28in (1100 x 700mm) clear floor space to dry yourself by the bath or to wash a child who is still in it. A space of 31 x 24in (800 x 600mm) is needed in front of the wc. There is no need to take the figures too seriously – and every need to take your own physical peculiarities into account – but they are useful to any bathroom planner.

The classic compact bathroom solution is the shower. It saves both hot water and space. But a bath is not simply functional. It is one of life's pleasures, as the old Romans understood. In modern Japan bathers wash and soap themselves

The bathroom on the facing page is one of a number of designs Manfred Wolff Plottegg has devised for the same small space. The room measures only 39 x 55in (1 x 1.4m). The perspective-distorting stripes confuse the sense of space in a room which would otherwise feel extremely cramped.

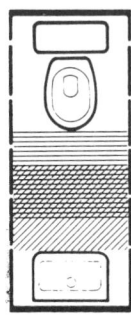

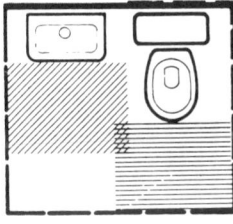

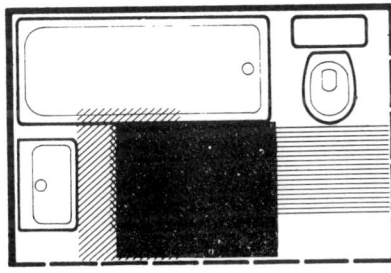

The standardization of bathroom fittings and laundry equipment has simplified bathroom design. Unfortunately, people do not all come in standard sizes. Nevertheless, studies of how much room you need to carry out certain functions in comfort can be useful, as long as you take your own peculiarities into account. In bathrooms, it is particularly important to remember that they may be used by children, who cannot reach standard fittings. The drawings on this page show some of the ergonomists' observations and conclusions, based on the standard human. (All measurements are given in millimetres.)

Top right: maximum, average, and minimum dimensions of a washing machine.

Centre right: the space you need to wash your face.

Below: the space you need to use the WC.

Bottom right: the space you need to towel yourself after a bath.

Left: suggested layouts of small bathrooms, with and without a bath.

The plans are taken from the UK Department of the Environment's Space in the Home, a follow-up to the influential Homes for Today and Tomorrow, which attempted to lay down new minimum standards in the 1960s.

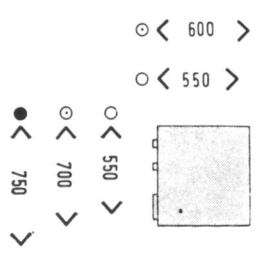

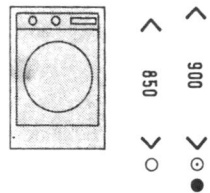

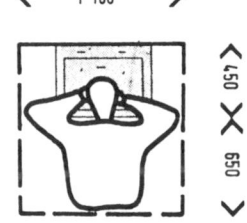

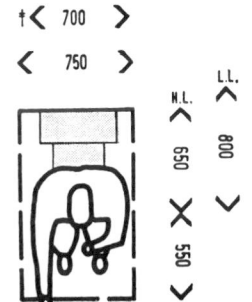

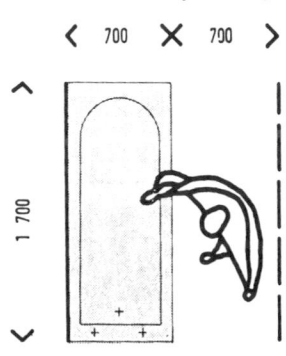

clean *before* they enter the bath, which is used simply for the joys of soaking. This admirable habit often causes confusion in western hotels, when Japanese guests leave the bathroom floor mysteriously flooded. If you share the Japanese delight in relaxing in baths, the space is worth taking. Small baths can be found and fitted into extremely small spaces, as the plans (page 47) show.

This remarkable room is only 39in (1m) wide. The use of perspective-distorting tiles set in the stark white walls makes it feel quite spacious.

The standard bath is 66in (1700mm) long, but 54in (1400mm) models are relatively easy to find, although only in a limited range. Small baths designed for the disabled are often fitted into awkward corners of caravans. The bath and shower area shown in the drawing is only 36in (900mm) square, only some 6in (150mm) larger than a typical shower tray, and offers both worlds: you can sit and soak in it or stand under a shower.

If you insist on cast iron, you may have to look for older models. Secondhand baths of all vintages and in good condition are available from the growing number of architectural salvage yards rescuing, restoring and selling the original fittings from demolished houses. Avoid old baths with damaged enamel, as re-enamelling is rarely a complete success.

For safety reasons there is a ban on normal wall-mounted light switches in the bathroom; only the pull-cord ceiling-mounted switch is acceptable. For the same reasons,

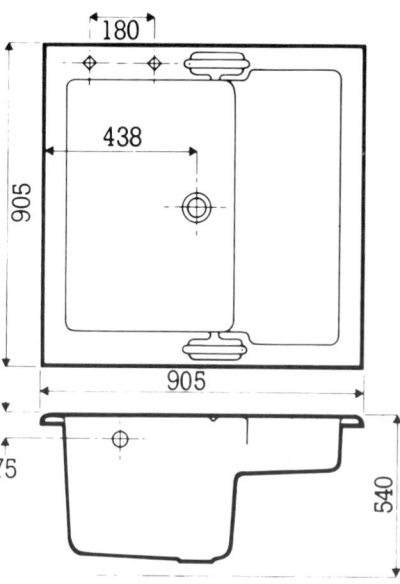

Baths like the one above can be fitted in the corner of a small bathroom. With the complete unit below an entire bathroom can be built into any corner.

socket outlets are not allowed in the bathroom. Health considerations have caused the planners to demand that there should be at least two doors between a kitchen and the only bathroom.

For your own health and comfort, it is unwise to place a bath under a window, where down-draughts can blow cold and where the bath will make opening, closing and cleaning the window a tricky operation. Bathrooms do not have to have a window to the outside, and internal bathrooms can be warmer and less liable to condensation. They can also be easier to design into your small space.

Modern fittings can ease your problems. Small low-level cisterns are available for wcs; the primitive high-level cistern can be a space-saver at floor level, allowing the lavatory to be fixed against the wall. They can also look right in old houses. Corner basins are small, but any small hand-basin can be a false economy, as they can be grotesquely difficult to use when you want to wash anything more than your hands in them. Save space by recessing fittings such as soap trays and lavatory-roll holders into the wall. Soggy towels are not user-friendly in any bathroom; consider fitting a heated towel rail.

Standard panels are available to clad the side of baths, but custom design provides the option of using the large space under the bath for storage, for example of cleaning materials.

The ancient Roman skills in bathroom design live on in Italy. One standard Italian solution to the bathroom problem is to create a waterproof room covered entirely in tiles, making a shower tray unnecessary. The tiled floor shelves towards a drain outlet set in the floor. A similar system could provide you with a sauna in the bathroom. Standard saunas are 5 x 7ft (1500 x 2100mm), but prefabricated units as small as 3 x 4ft (900 x 1200mm) are available.

Designers have been attracted by the idea of the prefabricated bathroom for decades. Buckminster Fuller was stimulated by designs for ships and aircraft when he developed his 420lb (190kg) one-piece, pressed-steel Dymaxion bathroom from research for the American Radiator Company in 1931. It never went into mass production, the manufacturers apparently fearing hostility from plumbing interests objecting to the fact that people could simply unplug their entire bathroom, move it to their new home and plug in again.

Many prefabricated bathrooms are on the market today, mainly aimed at the hotel industry. The ingenious one in the photograph (opposite) claims to be the smallest possible, fitting across the corner of a room, an idea small bathroom designers might imitate. The high lip encloses an area which can be used as both floor and bath.

The prefabricated bathroom was used by the French designer Charlotte Perriand – an early and important associate of Le Corbusier – in her designs for moutain ski resorts at Les Arcs between 1967 and 1982. She herself lives in a tiny but wonderful apartment in Paris, a

Above: Borrowing public space to dry washing in Italy. Equipment like the washer, which will take a load of 4.4lbs (2kg), and dryer (3lbs; 1.5kg) below makes more sense in the UK and the USA.

pleasing example of an architect practising what she preaches.

The bathroom can be the site of other activities, from a gymnasium to a laundry. Although the local laundromat is the obvious answer to the laundry problem, it is all too likely to depress you, leave you with odd socks and turn your white shirts grey. A washing machine of your own brings new freedom. The kitchen and bathroom are usually the most logical places to plumb in the washing machine, as they will already have the water supply and drainage on which the machine relies. Some machines save space by combining washer and dryer in the same box. Others are extremely small, such as the polypropylene plug-in countertop model in the photograph (left). This machine also saves time – the washing cycle takes only five minutes. It fills from the hot tap and drains through the sink outlet, so no special plumbing is needed.

Lines of damp and dripping clothes can make a place feel very cheerless. If you are forced to dry clothes indoors, an automatic dryer vented to the outside is desirable. At far lower cost, there is a wide choice of small, lightweight, portable plastic drying racks which span the bath and fold away after use.

Colourful lines of drying clothes spanning the street like bunting are a common sight in Italy. Simple mechanisms allow the clothes to be hauled out from an upper-storey window to dry out of the way in the open air. Similar systems can be used in areas sharing Italy's sunny climate.

Hard-line space-savers have strong views on furniture in small rooms. Everything which has only one function, they state, is probably redundant. This can lead to an obsession with folding furniture and gadgetry. It can also lead to a creative use of the same space for two or more functions.

An already crowded living-room may have to serve as an office, computer room or sewing area, while a bathroom may double as a photographic darkroom. Health-conscious Americans who are too busy to spend perhaps an hour going to and from their gymnasium are increasingly fitting home gyms into the bathroom. New compact gym equipment is making such a double use of the bathroom increasingly practical, allowing the owner to leap straight from a punishing workout into a muscle-soothing bath or shower. It is also easier for those with low-level motivation to lift weights or push exercise bicycles in a warm bathroom on a cold winter morning than to set off to the gym before work.

Where space is limited, the stationary exercise bicycle and the rowing machine are popular choices of equipment. These machines can be packed away in a closet or hung on the wall after the workout.

The multiple use of space is not an invention of space-conscious Manhattan. In traditional Islamic houses, a space may serve different purposes from season to season. The clearest example is the use of the flat roof as a bedroom in the summer.

Periodic religious rituals can be very demanding of space in city-centre Jewish homes, where there is, for example, little room for a permanent Passover kitchen. The problem has been solved in New York by the conversion of a tiny Brooklyn bedroom into a Passover kitchen which for most of the year is covered by folding wooden panels, allowing the room to be used as a study.

Perhaps the most inspiring Christian examples of multiple use of space are seen in the many paintings of St Jerome in his study, at work on his great Latin translation of the Bible (right). Artists often invented enviable study-bedrooms for the scholar saint.

Designing a study bedroom for a Manhattan writer and his dog was the problem faced by Jean Weiner and Paul Shafer of Cobuild, an architectural practice specializing in small spaces and operating from a suitably compact office on Broadway. Their inventive solution (see page 53) repays study.

Steven Aronson was all too aware of the problems in his apartment, having suffered them for years before he called in the professionals. Cobuild believe this is sound practice. They recommend living in a space for a time before you brief a designer to alter it for you. Time, they think, makes you more knowledgeable about the space, and makes your ideas more realistic. They begin their work, as does Eva Jiricna (see pages 89-90), by finding the problem. Their clients are usually clear about what they do not like about a space, less certain about what to do about it.

Honesty with the designer is crucial. It is relatively easy to say that the existing bed is too small, or that there is not enough room for your child's toys or your collection of strange objects. It is just as important to say that you spend your evenings watching television.

Having established the general principles, detailed work can begin. They pay particular attention to the views within an apartment, what you see when you walk into the room and when you are sitting down or eating. They are skilled in using the diagonals within a room, which are the longest vista through the typical apartment.

Lighting is also an important element. Many of their schemes involve the construction of substantial cabinetry, and to simplify lighting and other electrical wiring, they run the cable through the new structures.

Cobuild's approach is instructive and encouraging. Your small space, they believe, will never be a palace, but it can be a wonderful space. Too often, people are prevented from maximizing the potential of a small apartment by worrying too much about good taste. A living space is not purely functional. You have to enjoy being there.

Paintings of Saint Jerome are a wonderful source of ideas for study bedrooms (pets allowed – his lion is usually somewhere about). This one is by Hugo van Steenwyck. Note the raised plinths keeping draughts at bay and the built-in furniture, which has a lesson: a modern chair can look good in an old room but built-in cupboards may look odd if they do not acknowledge the room's details.

It appears to be one of the laws of the universe that possessions will expand beyond the capacity of storage systems to hold them. Packing things into minimal storage space is the key art in compact living, a fact which has prompted the British navy to produce a training film on the tricks of stowage to teach the submarine service how best to use every odd corner of the boat.

In the limited space of the submarine every cubic inch must be used. Drawers slide out of walls at odd angles, ceiling panels are removed to reveal kit stores, stool seats lift on hinges to reveal document files – indeed, the stools are designed around the size of a standard file – and panels in the floor are raised to give access to food storage beneath.

People living in caravans also exploit the underfloor space for storage, and similar strategies can increase storage space in any house. Safes are often set into the space between the flooring joists, and storage boxes – which must be fireproof – can be built into floors. Support between the joists will be needed to stop your store dropping on the neighbours below. To gain access, the floorboards must be lifted, and the recessed catches, handles and hinges sold by boat chandlers are specifically designed for a flush-fitting job. Once again, a good boat chandler's catalogue is well worth examining in the hunt for space-saving ideas.

The joists can also support an overhead storage system, which is useful for long, awkward items such as the timber waiting to be converted into a storage system, a routine problem for do-it-yourselfers without a work room. A pair of rope slings or even two tyres on wires can be hung from the joists, but purpose-built metal brackets bolted to the joists will look more elegant. If access is a problem, your model could be the old overhead clothes rail, raised and lowered by a rope-and-pulley system.

Examine every part of your space for storage potential. The space under stairs should not be unused. Panelling under the stairs can be removed to open up the area, but a system of flush-fitting boxes on wheels, rolling out of the panels, can be very tidy. The boxes can be built by mounting a platform on four castors, topping it with a cupboard and guiding the assembly by wood nailed to the floor.

The space in an entrance hall is often underexploited. In traditional row or terraced houses the basement hallway is routinely converted to use as a dining area. The photographs on page 114 show a practical adaptation of the hall by New York architect Richard R. Lewis. He designed a built-in contemporary version of the old drop-front desk to create an instant office in the entrance hall of a Manhattan apartment.

The space inside a partition wall can be exploited for storage of shallow items such as cassette tapes. A simple and neat method of opening up the wall is explained on page 30.

Before constructing any closets or shelves, measure your belongings. Many will be standard sizes, others will be odd. Standard items will include audio and video cassette tapes, records, bottles and – up to a point – shoes and books. Efficient shelving can be planned around the dimensions of your current possessions, although it is always wise to allow for the almost inevitable future expansion.

Some awkward items can be accommodated by putting them on display rather than trying to hide them behind closet doors. Fishing tackle, a bicycle or skis, for example, can be hung from the wall or ceiling, out of the way, on a pair of metal brackets which are manufactured specially for the job. A folding bicycle will, of course, save space in the home as well as on the commuter train. The folding baby buggy, which has eclipsed the traditional pram, is another modern product helping to ease the pressure in the closet.

Choosing possessions in the smallest available version can help, as long as they work. Indeed, it makes sense not to buy any big books for small spaces – leave them in the library. Some small-space livers have donated their books to chosen libraries, where they can still consult them without having to store them, and gain the added kudos of being a benefactor. If you own some bulky volumes, store them flat on shallow shelves, two or three high. The largest books look best if they are on the bottom shelves, and storing the heaviest books on the lower shelves improves the stability of a free-standing bookcase.

Only the most serious booklovers can afford to build up a general library in a small space. Throwing

STORAGE

Industrial and office storage catalogues contain many space-saving items adaptable to home use. These examples are from the Key Industrial Equipment mail order catalogue. The photographs show a modular steel and wood platform with a safety rail and stairway designed by Keith Hancock Structures for erection by the unskilled (below, right), an adaptable S.I.M.A. shelving system, which is easily and quickly assembled without tools (below, left) and a flat-pack collapsible Light Alloy container, with all parts hinged together for easy storage(bottom left, centre and right).

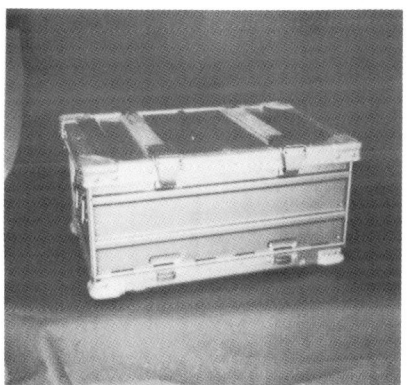

Built-in and system storage comes in dozens of shapes, sizes and prices. The principles are usually pretty much the same, however. Frames, slotted planks, vertical rails or (as in the example illustrated left and right by Manhattan architect Richard H. Lewis) the sides of a niche – support shelf, cabinet and drawer modules. The advantages are that no part of the supporting wall need be wasted, and the size of the unit can be adapted to it. In a small space, however, a whole wall of storage makes what is already small, smaller, and a wall of cupboards reaching nearly to the ceiling looms over you. If you are building-in, measure first (if all your bookshelves are big enough for your largest volumes you will waste space above the paperbacks), and do not make shelves deeper than they need be. Drop-front desk units like the one shown here are fine for signing the odd cheque, but for real work you want to get your knees under the desk and a drop-front that projects far enough is exceptional.

old newspapers and magazines away is not a hard discipline. Reference books clearly deserve a place on the shelves, since they are often used, but paperback novels are rarely reread, and another copy can always be bought or borrowed. On purely practical grounds, the novels should be sold or given to charity, but many readers identify closely with old books and use them like the old diaries in the drawer as a route into the past. If books are important to you, you will need a lot of shelves to hold them.

To calculate how much shelving your books demand, measure your present collection in linear feet or metres, then add on a generous

percentage for future acquisitions. One simple method of maximizing book storage is to have double-depth shelves. Shelves 12in (300mm) deep can take two layers of books, which can mean bookshelves along only one wall rather than two.

Whether you choose built-in or free-standing bookcases, massing the shelves along one wall is the simplest method. A professional version of the double-depth shelf is the bank of safe-like closets used in library stacks, laid parallel on their long sides and set in ceiling and floor tracks.

Industrial steel shelves will not sag under the considerable weight of paper. The steel shelf provides an

inexpensive solution to book and record storage, and is often more practical than built-in shelving in rented spaces since it does not require any wall fixings, which might upset a sensitive landlord, and you can take it with you when you leave.

The professional approach to storage design begins by cataloguing all the possessions to be stored. Only then can the designer decide how much drawer space is needed, how many bookshelves and how much closet space.

Building more closets may seem the obvious answer to the problem of bulging closets, but this is often impractical. In rental apartments it could be a poor investment, and even those who own their homes may be reluctant to invest either their limited space or limited money in an expensive new system.

If you decide in favour of extra closets, consider their impact on the shape of the room. You can improve the shape of a room by constructing a shallow floor-to-ceiling closet along the full length of a wall.

A more efficient use of the existing closet space can improve matters dramatically. Begin at the doors. On old closets, doors are often not the full width of the closet. Widening them improves access to dark corners. Folding or sliding doors may make better use of space than hinged doors.

Many of the clothes hanging in the closet – jackets, blouses, shirts and skirts for example – are short and can be hung in two tiers in the closet. By raising the existing hanging rail and adding a second rail below, the storage capacity is instantly doubled. Incidentally, hangers slide more easily on metal rather than on wood.

Men's suits and overcoats demand a space of 24in (600mm). On airlines, where space is valuable, jackets are stored face-on, with only the front garment on view, to save space. By adding a telescopic rack to the closet, you have access to all the clothes without contortions. Knitwear may stretch if it is hung up. It can be folded flat and kept on shelves or in drawers. Both shelves and drawers will slide out of the closet for access.

Unplanned shoe storage can be cumbersome and untidy. Shoes can

be kept on racks or hung in bags behind the closet door. The space behind doors should be fully exploited, for accessories such as ties, belts and scarves.

Small spaces call for disciplined living. Accessible storage could be occupied only by the clothes you are likely to wear this season, while off-season garments are boxed and stored away, perhaps under the bed. The greatest and most difficult discipline is to discard any clothes which you have not worn for, say, two years, since they can be judged no longer to justify house room.

An instant rearrangement can be achieved by fitting one of the inexpensive, purpose-made closet

A two-tier drawer (below) maximizes convenient use of a limited space. A wide range of space-saving drawer and cabinet fittings – carousel trays and baskets, telescopic rails, extending tables, foldaway mixer fittings or ironing boards disguised as drawers, pull-out garbage bins and larders – can be bought by mail order from furniture fittings suppliers and incorporated in compact kitchen design.

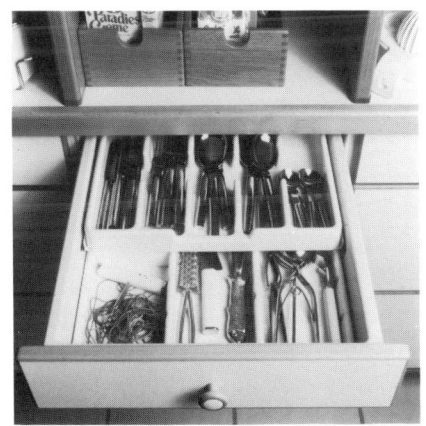

kits, made in various sizes. These systems are extremely flexible, and can be adapted as your wardrobe changes. They can also be taken with you when you move. The accessory catalogues are packed with useful ideas, from folding skirt racks to sliding baskets.

Office equipment catalogues are another source of storage ideas. Anyone considering constructing simple and practical rolling platforms for example could explore industrial equipment catalogues for castors and other heavy-metal fittings suitable for home use.

At the lighter end of storage is the fabric storage system, familiar from aircraft, where an elasticated fabric pocket is mounted behind each seat. The storage possibilities of your furniture should not be ignored. On the space shuttle, storage bags are held to the walls by strips of hook-and-loop fastener (Velcro). In the Skylab days, Velcro was used extensively. It was even stuck on the backs of the cutlery, pens and pads to stop them floating away towards the ventilation system. The astronauts' suits are covered in Velcro, turning them into a mobile extension of the storage system.

Space-saving storage is crucial on the shuttle. As on the submarine, everything has to be on board before blast-off, enough to supply a crew of seven for up to a month. They use under-floor storage and a battery of lockers, with hinged doors hiding drawers, many of them fitted out like a photographer's case with cut foam moulds to prevent equipment rattling around as they hurtle in orbit.

Packing possessions into a limited space at home is a large-scale version of the routine problems the traveller faces when packing suitcases for a journey – how can it possibly all fit in without crushing the contents or exploding the case? Packing is an art, and many of the techniques developed by the world's professional packers and luggage makers can help home storage organization.

The Parisian firm Louis Vuitton is the most distinguished name in luxury luggage. They have over 130 years' experience in making ingenious luxury luggage for fashionable travellers. The best Vuitton pieces are simple in construction but brilliant in conception. The principle guiding the company through its long history is one worth following in a compact space – custom design. They take any object and design the package around it, whether it is a travelling music cabinet for the orchestral scores of Maestro Leopold Stokowski, wicker trunks for the Sultan of Egypt's fresh fruit, a case for Claude François' guitar or an attaché case with a false bottom for someone with something to hide.

They also consider available space. In the days of glamorous transatlantic steamer crossings, they designed a cabin trunk for Calouste S. Gulbenkian which slid neatly under the berth in his cabin. The idea was immediately hijacked by other manufacturers. Borrowing ideas from Vuitton is a century-old tradition, and the forgers are still hard at work supplying markets from North Africa to the Far East with fake Vuittons.

Three originals by Louis Vuitton, in each case a box carefully matched to its contents. They range in date from 1875 to 1936: the secretaire specially made for Leopold Stokowski (above), the wardrobe/trunk which was in regular demand from 1875 onwards (opposite, bottom) and a tool box, custom-made to fit on the running-board of a motor car (opposite, top).

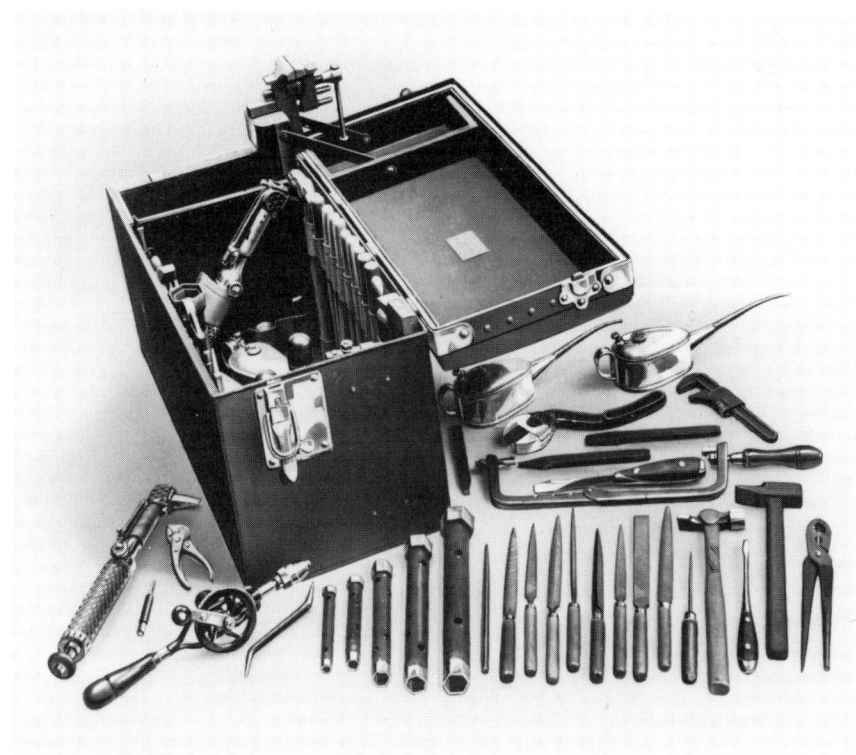

The secretaire designed for the conductor Leopold Stokowski in 1936 opens to reveal bookshelves, typewriter compartment and drawers for documents and musical scores. The hinged writing table folds into the door. The bookshelves slot into any of seven pairs of grooves, making them impressively adjustable.

The motorist's tool box (above right) made in 1908 was, like so many Vuitton creations, designed to fit a specific space, in this case the right hand running board of the car. A matching box on the left hand side held spare parts.

Faced with the difficulties of fitting his vast travelling trunk into a poky cabin at the start of the chaotic transatlantic steamer crossing in *Night at the Opera*, Groucho Marx asked the steward 'would it not be easier to fit the room in the trunk?' As early as 1903 Vuitton was designing trunks which almost fitted the bill. The Ideal trunk (below) had compartments for five men's suits, one overcoat,

eighteen shirts, four pairs of shoes, linen, a hat, three walking sticks and an umbrella. Internal dividers slotted inside the trunk drawers improve organization. The design principle is still valid – decide what the storage space must hold before you design it.

The classic Louis Vuitton wardrobe has hardly changed since it was first made in 1875. Internal divisions are slotted into the drawers, whose soft leather handles are a feature of Vuitton luggage. The attache case which stands in the bottom of the wardrobe in transit can be lifted out and used independently. The front bar holding the clothes hangers in position unfolds to allow the hangers (which sit on rods at each side) to be drawn forward.

New York loft livers are now buying these Vuitton trunks for home use. Strong hinges are necessary if such a weighty object is to be hung from the wall.

The wardrobe shows the extremely useful, space-saving refrigerator principle – the store in the door, a key concept in small-space storage. It is worth getting up early in Paris to see the opening of the press kiosks on the Parisian boulevards. They unfold to reveal a bewilderingly large stock inside.

There's rarely room for a mammoth 1950s jukebox in a tiny apartment. We are condemned to use the compact disc player and other mini-equipment. It is extraordinary to consider how much space the equipment made for the home-based music lovers of thirty years ago – in the days before the audio and video tape cassette and the compact disc – would have needed in order to supply them with a multi-band radio, tape recorder/player, television and facilities to watch movies at home.

Modern technology has improved the standard of entertainment in the small space. A personal stereo cassette player is now a routine item for the members of the submarine crew, and the video cassette recorder has made it possible to view films in the confined space of the submarine wardroom, replacing the whirring of the film projector aimed at the back of a chart hung on the wall.

Some submarine crews have installed car cassette players in their wardrooms. These small and robust machines are ideal for submarine conditions and take up little space when built into a storage system at home.

Home electronic equipment continues to shrink, packing high quality sound reproduction into ever smaller spaces. While the compact systems cannot match the performance of the giants, some good sound equipment will now fit comfortably on bookshelves 10in (50mm) deep. Even the compact disc player is growing smaller. By 1986 a CD player only 5 x 5 x 1in (125 x 125 x 25mm) was on sale.

Mini sound systems are designed for small spaces, with components no more than 9in (225mm) deep.

The new mini audio systems are in the finest Japanese traditions of miniaturization and are ideal for small spaces, where the power of mammoth speakers would be wasted. The system below (left) offers a respectable thirty watts per channel through its three-way speakers and claims the world's smallest auto-reverse double cassette deck. As equipment shrinks it becomes more mobile. Sony have followed the ubiquitous Walkman with more miniatures (below) for the walking media addict – the Diskman CD player measuring just 5 × 5¼ × 1½ in (125 × 130 × 40mm) and the Watchman, a battery-operated television set 6 × 2½ × 1½in (157 × 54 × 42mm), weighing 14½oz (410g). If you are carrying your entire home and furniture on your back, low bulk is important. Camping catalogues are therefore a rich source of space-saving ideas, as the illustrations opposite, from the Campmor catalogue, prove.

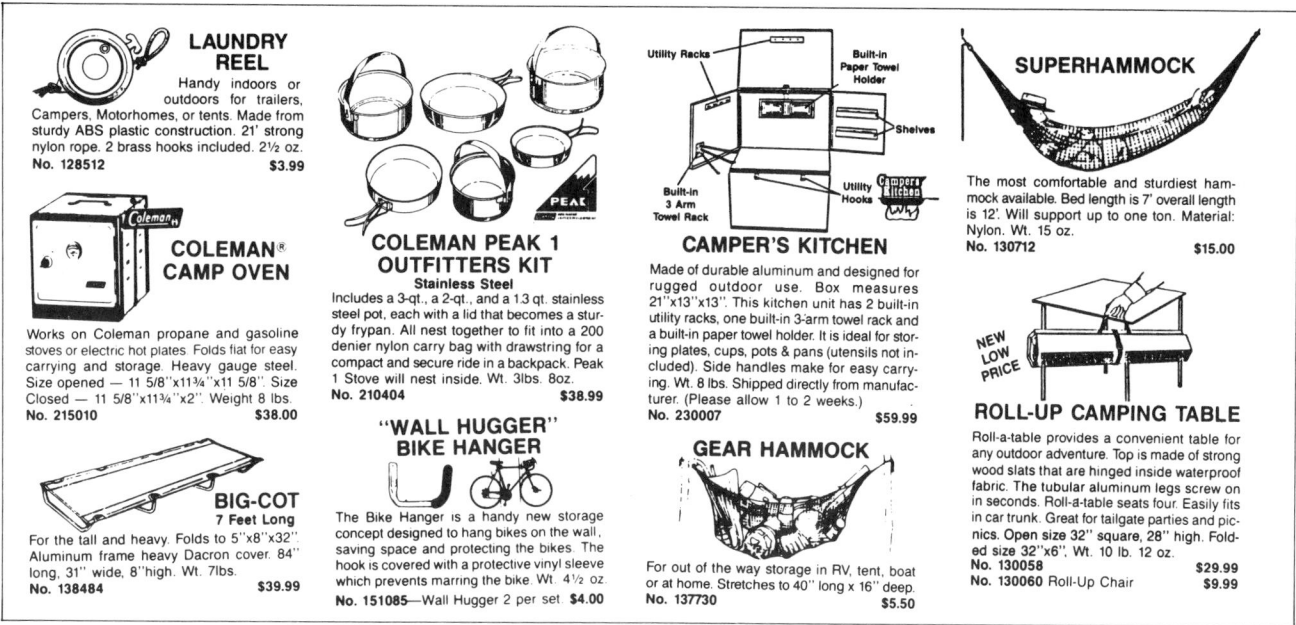

These now offer such desirable features as a digital AM/FM tuner, both a CD player and a conventional turntable with a radial tracking arm, an auto-reverse cassette deck, a powered amplifier giving 75 watts per channel, and speakers. And all this can be operated by remote control.

Even more space-conscious is the Japanese system designed to hang out of the way on the wall. The entire unit is under 3in (75mm) thick, which makes it possible to set the unit inside a partition wall by the method described on page 30. The system's slim speakers are mounted separately, but these too can be wall hung.

Reducing speaker size without impairing quality is the greatest challenge for the designers. Many small speakers will not reproduce symphonic sounds with any warmth. It is therefore essential to listen to the speakers before buying them.

The stereo system may soon be joined on the wall by the television set. Already the excellent Pivotelli bracket allows wall mounting, but the next generation of flat screen sets will upgrade the entertainment possibilities in the very smallest spaces. The designers of such equipment have concentrated on making it as unobtrusive as it is small, with features including flat slide controls rather than bulky knobs.

If you are carrying your home on your back you need more than a snail does, light weight and low bulk count, whether you are on camping holiday or marching to war, the two rountine in-tent situations. A lot of inexpensive equipment developed for campers is useful at home, if only as a design model. The sleeping bags, camp beds, and inflatable mattresses in camping catalogues are classic space-saving beds to bring out for an unexpected guest. Between the ads for skunk repellent and snake-bite extractors, the catalogues display an astonishing range of equipment which folds flat or rolls up for easy carriage when camp is struck. Some foldaway stoves are very sophisticated and not as ugly as their style-free predecessors.

On the storage front, fabric larders and wardrobes can hang in tents from hooks, alongside a dangling clothes rack. Fabric storage systems fitted with pockets, are manufactured for home use, and offer similar advantages in home or camp — when the moment comes to move, it all folds neatly away.

The dog-leg staircase rising through the standard town house since the eighteenth century is a major space eater, typically taking up a quarter of the ground plan. Redesigning the stairs can free large spaces.

Radical solutions can be contemplated, such as a staircase outside the house, an idea familiar from New York fire escapes and used in a very contemporary context by Japanese architect Tadao Ando (see page 24) in his concrete house.

The most minimal solution for a small space is the fireman's pole, but it is extremely hard to climb up. The lift – whose invention was partly responsible for the skyscraper – works both up and down (if it is working at all), but is normally too expensive for home use.

Ladders can be useful for access to attic spaces or platform beds. Aluminium ladders are used to reach the top bunk in railroad sleeping cars. On the luxury Orient Express the ladder is padded and covered in fabric matching the upholstery throughout the compartment. Buyers should beware of old ladders, particularly painted ones, as paint can hide dangerous cracks and splits in rungs and stiles.

The most practical alternative to the traditional staircase is the spiral, a space-saving design from the medieval castle now widely used for fire escapes, in London's underground stations and on intercontinental aircraft, where space is too expensive to waste and where a spiral staircase leads up to the first-class lounge. The spiral can be open, as the photograph of the staircase designed by architect Pierre Botschi (opposite) shows. Before installing a spiral, be sure that you will be able to manoeuvre bulky furniture up and down the new stairs.

Opening up the existing stairs creates more visual space. Replacing a boxed-in staircase with open treads supported only in the wall can be an expensive undertaking, and local building codes may outlaw the idea. The space under the stairs is often underused and easily opened up. Successful uses of the understair space include storage, bathroom, office or telephone table.

The stairs themselves can be used for storage. Drawers can be fitted in the side of the stairs, an idea used centuries ago in Japan and seen in the Viennese bachelor flat in the photograph (right). Designed by Franz Singer in the 1930s, the flat incorporated the latest Modern Movement space-saving ideas. As well as the use of the cavities under the stairs for an array of drawers and cupboards, there is a folding door, nesting chair and stool and a sofa bed which folds up against the wall.

The stairs in Eva Jiricna's small flat (pages 87–90) offer a versatile solution for the small space. The stairs are built from a number of independent stacked boxes, which can be used for storage and provide additional seating at dinner.

A metal-tube platform with a minimal staircase of the same material designed by Pierre Botschi (opposite). In the Viennese flat by Franz Singer in the 1930s (right) and the Japanese house drawn by Edward Morse in the 1870s (below, right), drawers and cupboards are fitted under staircases.

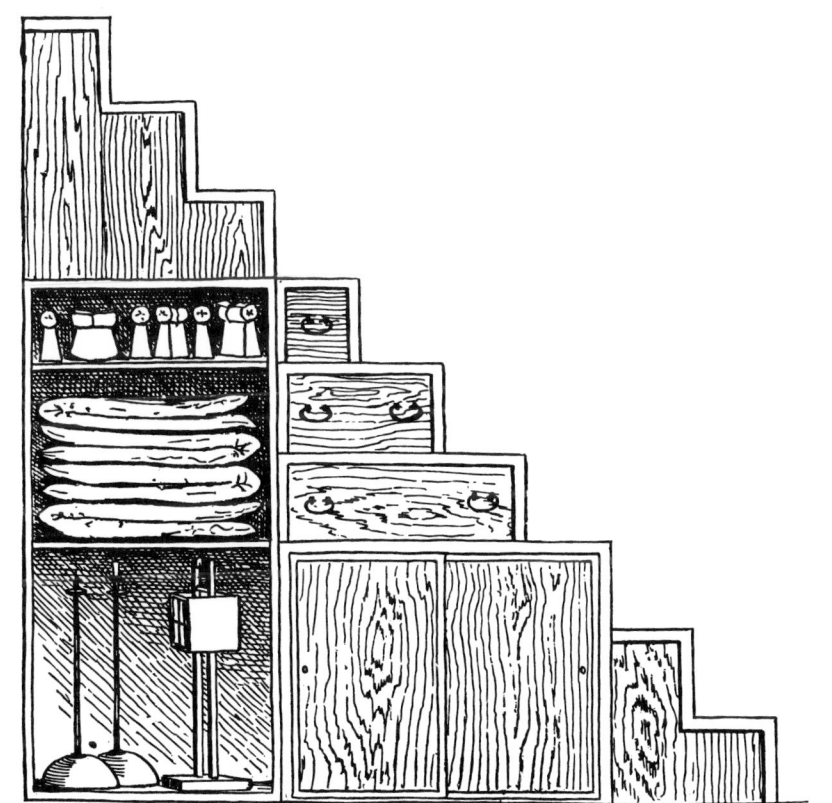

121

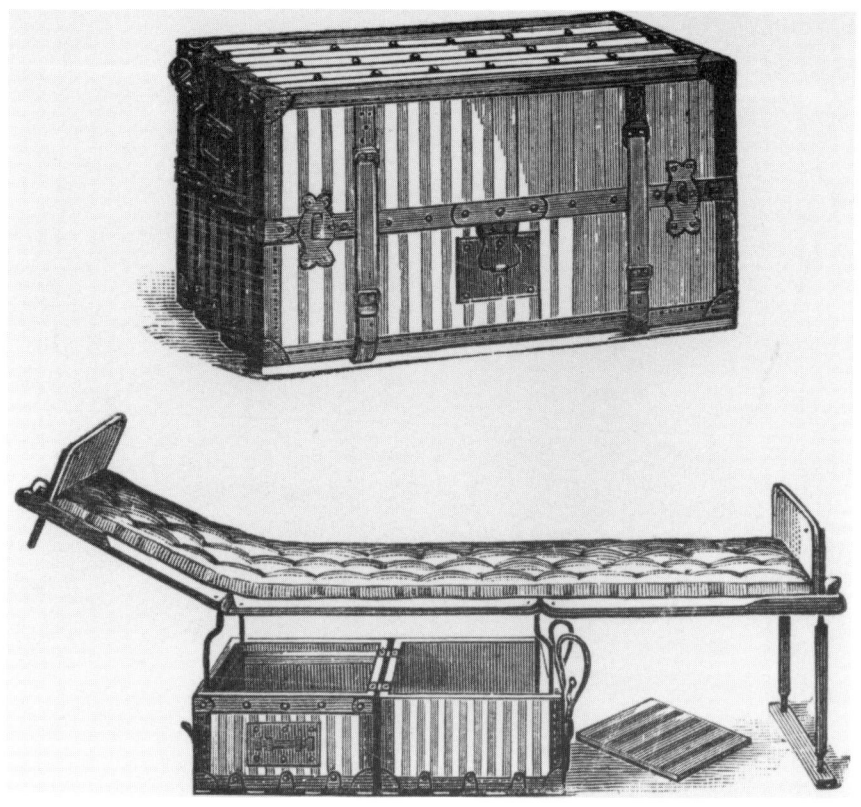

A traditional bed is a bulky item, but efforts to economize on the considerable floor area it occupies should not tempt you to ruin your sleep on an uncomfortable surface. You can, without guilt, impose space-saving sleeping arrangements on overnight guests. A permanent guest-room is recognized as a rare luxury in a small house or apartment. When a guest stays, the hammock, inflatable mattress and camp bed can come out of the closet. Camp beds, which go back to the folding beds slept on by the armies of the Roman empire, too often bear the spartan traces of their military origins. Fortunately, Danish

designers, among others, have recently improved the looks, width and comfort of the military model.

The Japanese futon (opposite) is an increasingly popular form of folding bed. Unrolled on the bedroom floor, its low profile makes it unobtrusive in the small space. Futon manufacturers claim that their product calms aching backs, by providing just the right amount of support for the spine, allowing the body to relax without sinking into unhealthy positions in an over-soft mattress. However, the futon will absorb body moisture and can soon become undesirably damp, even mouldy, if it is not properly aired.

Bear in mind that even the cleanest sleeper can be oozing over a pint of moisture into the bed each night, and this can quickly accumulate.

Following the Japanese example of rolling up the futon during the day and giving it a regular airing reduces the risk of damp and prevents the body's contours becoming permanently imprinted in the futon. The need to lift the futon makes it unwise to buy some of the thick and extremely heavy futons sold to the western public. Western futons are often raised on a low slatted platform, which improves both ventilation and access.

No low mattress is easy to use when you are old, injured or ill. An adjustable bed such as the one by the German company Frogdesign tackles this awkward problem by allowing the sleeper to raise the bed level as he or she grows less supple.

Raising the bed creates storage space beneath. Underbed drawers on castors can be bought to adapt an existing bed. One of the most logical items to store under the bed is another bed (see photograph, right). Beds-under-the-bed are in a tradition going back to the truckle bed of the Middle Ages.

While futons were spending their days in the closets of Japan, the rising sun saw American closet doors closing on the famous fold-up Murphy bed (see page 124), the star of countless silent movie disaster scenes and of the crucial opening sequence of the James Bond movie *You Only Live Twice*. The family-owned Murphy company is now run by the inventor's grandson. The original Mr Murphy's creation was of

Louis Vuitton's folding camp bed (opposite), as used by the explorer de Brazza in his travels in the Congo, came complete with mattress, blankets and four sheets. The truckle bed which rolls under a larger one – the main bed was commonly the master's and the truckle the servant's – is an idea which goes back to the Middle Ages. It is revived in its essentials in the twin beds below – wheels can be seen on the right-hand unit of the pair. The futon (right) originated in Japan, where it was used without a bed-base. Hard beds may well be better for your back: they are certainly less bulky and easier to put up and take down than soft ones. All these well-tried solutions make sense in small spaces and exist in modern versions. Camping equipment catalogues list folding beds (see page 119), and increasing numbers of futon makers are to be found in Europe and America.

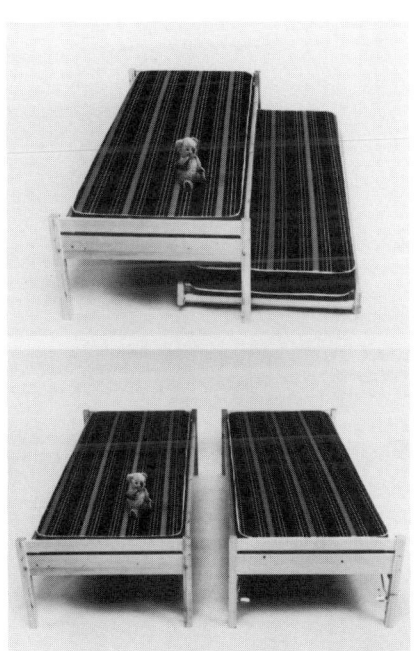

its time. Similar beds were beginning to pop out of cupboards and walls in Europe through the 1920s and 1930s. The architect Erich Mendelsohn, for instance, built a pair into the guest room of his Berlin flat, complete with lights over the beds and a pull-out bedside table.

The bed-in-a-closet is much older than the Murphy Door Bed Co. Inc. of Amityville. Beds incorporated in both freestanding and built-in cupboards are common throughout rural Europe, providing a degree of privacy in crowded cottages. The beds in the space shuttle follow a similar pattern.

The main block of 'sleep stations' on the shuttle is a bank of three bunks. The bunk is a practical way of raising the bed off the floor when there is not enough headroom in the bedroom to allow the construction of a platform. It is particularly popular in children's rooms.

Low ceilings normally rule out the platform bed – a minimum ceiling height of 12ft (3.6m) is normally recommended to allow room for a platform construction without the risk of head banging, but a satisfactory Japanese-style room can be constructed either under the platform or on it. Other low activities, such as sitting at a desk and working, may also be fitted under or over the platform. There are many patterns for do-it-yourself platform beds made of wood, but far fewer use metal. Metal can look good, as Ferrari's iron platform in Milan proves (see page 70). Metal scaffold is a versatile and handsome material ideally suited to platform construction.

BEDS

Ron Arad's 'Platform C' bed is made of tubular steel. The joints are cast-iron and the mattress is supported by structural steel mesh. An aluminium venetian blind hangs in front of the clothes-storage area. The bed-base projects beyond the outer upright and frees some of the floor space which is lost in the closet-underneath style of platform bed (below left).

The plinth of storage chests around the late fifteenth-century Italian bed (opposite) is admirable for those who hold levées, but has limitations as storage – certainly better for bedding than clothes. It also fails to use the space under the bed which can (as in the study-bedroom shown on page 84) take a substantial drawer.

A US-made Murphy bed (above) – open and closed. Murphy beds come (as television sets used to) in 'modern' and 'traditional' styles, but the mechanism is the same. Although the revelation scene is comical, this is a genuinely easy way of freeing the floor space taken up by a bed. Most foldaway beds are a trial if they have to be put up regularly.

The construction industry's heavy scaffolding will be considered rugged or ugly, according to taste. Chromium-plating achieves a spectacular improvement in the tube's looks, but costs will be horribly high. Stainless steel tubes can be polished professionally to a high shine.

If you buy lengths of builders' scaffold, they can be improved by paint. Your paint dealer should be able to recommend suitable paint for use on metal. Whatever paint you apply, it is important to remove all traces of rust and grease before you start painting.

Choose your clamps with care. The traditional crude, sharp industrial clamps are less suitable in most contexts than the neater Kee clamps, which are used on the bed platform by British designer Ron Arad (opposite left).

Arad's bed is becoming a modern classic. Below bed level is a large storage shelf. The area below can be used to hang clothes or to fit a small office. One of the advantages of Arad's design is that, unlike many imitations, it will fit in cars, through doors and up lifts and stairs. Oddly enough, Arad has never been thoroughly convinced by convertible furniture, which is a routine way of saving space. He thinks it makes you too active at home and rarely works perfectly as one thing or the other.

The sofa is probably the most popular hiding place for a bed these days, and a good alternative to the guest room, since it converts a sitting room into a comfortable temporary bedroom. Indeed, the best sofa beds are suitable for regular use. If two people are using the sofa bed as their main bed, it should be 5ft (1.5m) wide, although 4ft 6in (1.35m) is adequate for occasional double use.

There are two basic types of sofa bed – the traditional pull-outs with a proper mattress hidden inside the sofa and bracket-like legs emerging from the sofa thanks to a sophisticated mechanism, and the newer, inexpensive, foam flip-overs where the back of the seat becomes the bed. This type rarely has any mechanism.

Designs of the mechanized sofa bed have improved considerably since the shin-scarring heavyweights of the 1950s. In the modern convertible, aluminium and steel have replaced the heavy cast iron which made their predecessors so hard to move.

The convertible sofa bed is at the top end of the bed-seat market. Their independent mattress may be the same as the deep innerspring mattresses gracing the best conventional beds. The mattress can be replaced when it grows old, and the fabric covering can normally be removed for cleaning or replacement. It is wise to check whether this is possible before buying an expensive sofa bed.

It is also imperative to try out the folding mechanism, both ways, to see if it will be as convenient in use as you hope. Check also what the mattress is made of. It could be innerspring, foam or some other material. Test the weight of the sofa before you have to carry it upstairs, and see whether the frame is made of hardwood or a less expensive and less durable softwood. A warranty would be a useful safeguard against disaster.

Folding furniture has a long and distinguished history. The space-saving needs of armies have prompted the development of a wide range of collapsible camp beds, tables and cooking equipment, which can be bought from military surplus suppliers and camping catalogues. Folding chairs were on active service in the Napoleonic campaigns.

In spite of these very practical origins, as early as the 1920s the cartoons of Heath Robinson were mocking the modernist excesses of the furniture folders.

Seating which saves space: the 'Cricket' folding chair (above); an American writing chair from the 1780s (right, above) with an oval writing surface and drawer underneath, and the Balans chair (right, below) a recent and much praised kneeling chair which is kind to the back.

Furniture cannot solve all life's problems. It often *is* one of life's problems. However, an informed choice of furniture can save space without sacrificing comfort.

Low-level seating will increase a feeling of space, but is inappropriate for such normal western practices as eating around a dining table or working at a desk. Chairs can of course be multi-purpose. The kitchen chair can also be used for working, for example.

When you are choosing chairs, bear your dimensions in mind. The study of human dimensions has established certain standards for chair design. Experts often disagree, but many conclude that seat height should be no greater than the length of the lower leg, allowing you to place your feet flat on the floor. Depth should be less than the distance from the back of the buttock to the back of the knee. If the seat has arms, it should be wide enough to allow the sitter room to adjust position.

Professional designers have been working on the small-space problem for years. The result of their efforts is a mountain of folding furniture.

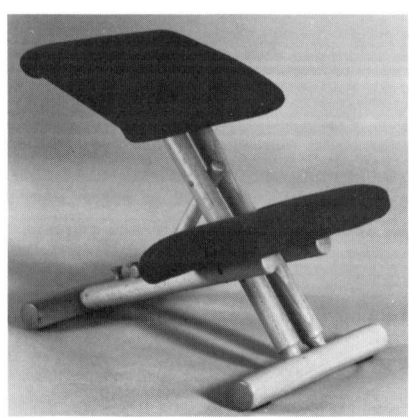

Pira's very slim folder (left) and Balans's very radical adjustable-height folder (below, left) make it possible to store attractive seating in very little space. Both these chairs look good enough to be hung on walls.

The Terna chair (right) can be folded flat by pulling apart the two frames which meet at the front of the seat. The steps (bottom) double as a stool. The pioneering inflatable Blow chair (below) either takes up a great deal of space, or can be stuffed in the back of the cupboard. In all these cases the fact that the pieces can be packed away is relevant if you really do have only occasional use for them, otherwise it may just be a nuisance.

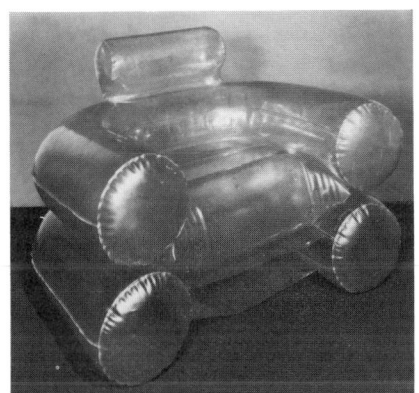

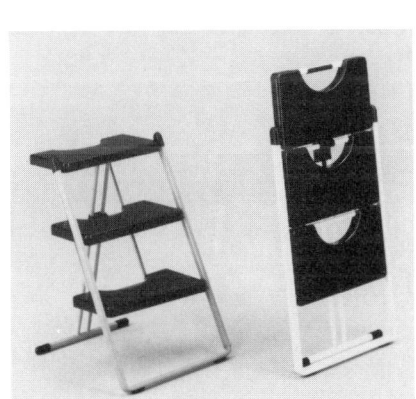

This mockery has failed to daunt the designers. Even in the high-tech space shuttle the seats are folded up and stowed away to save space in space when they reach orbit. Houses with zero gravity do not need chairs.

One of the most minimal

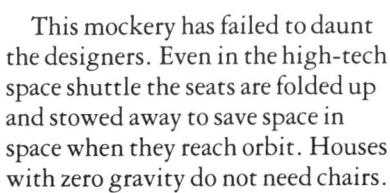

earthbound chairs is the shooting stick, which takes the weight off the racegoer's feet. It is also desirably dual-purpose, converting instantly to double as a walking stick. Some contemporary chairs are more comfortable, easily adjustable variants on the shooting stick.

The cheapest thing to sit on is your heels, and some argue that nobody needs chairs. The founder of the Alexander technique which has put an end to many sufferers' painful back problems claimed that chair design was relatively unimportant. 'We must educate the people, not the furniture,' he declared.

Folding chairs make sense in kitchen-diners where space is at a premium. Chairs can be hung out of the way on the wall and brought out only when needed. Not all folding chairs are as simple as their lines suggest. Assembly can be irritatingly tricky, more reminiscent of a gymnasium than a sitting-room.

The effort involved in chair conversion may soon be over. American manufacturers are making inexpensive 'motion furniture', motorized chairs which recline at the push of a button. A motor on the Thayer Coggins tub chair is activated to inflate the low back area, while the 'Cuddler' tilts sitters back and lifts them up.

Few multi-purpose seats work perfectly for all purposes. Ergonomic research suggests the multi-purpose should have a convex back. Seventeen inches (430mm) is both the recommended seat height and the recommended maximum seat depth. A pad of foam rubber over the whole seat is considered desirable.

There are many successful folding chairs for office and kitchen use, but folding easy chairs are not so easy to design. We all want to relax in an easy chair from time to time and read, doze, listen to music or watch television. A favorite easy chair can justify its presence in even the most crowded room.

Stacks of chairs in a Venetian square. Robust seating designed for restaurants, halls and churches usually stacks.

Activities as varied as eating, sewing, typing and drawing the plans of your small space usually take place on the horizontal surface of a table. It is an item of furniture you cannot do without. Whereas unused chairs can be folded up, hung on the wall or slotted in a closet to free floor space, the table is rarely out of action for long enough to justify the most temporary removal. Even when all other furniture is cleared away to create space for a party, the table still stands to carry the food and drink. Astronauts floated cheerfully in a chair-free environment on early manned space flights, but they soon missed the table, and one is now a standard fitting.

The traditional dining table can easily double as a working surface, but it can dominate a small space to an undesirable degree. Designers of small spaces generally advise against the large table in the middle of the room. Low-level tables are less obtrusive, even if they take up as much floor, and clear glass or plexiglass tops can reduce the visual impact of the table.

Convertible tables are an old solution to the problem of designing the all-purpose table, as the expression 'turning the tables on someone' indicates. The expression comes from the medieval practice of having a reversible table top on trestles, the rough side being used for everyday work and humble visitors, the polished surface being turned up only to greet the honoured guest.

Drop-leaf and gate-leg tables extend when necessary. Prices of even the most ordinary secondhand

extending-leaf tables have risen rapidly in recent years, as their versatility in small spaces is appreciated. These old models use a much simpler mechanism than some modern variations, which can be a mess of flexibility with too many legs kicking a tiny problem. The table standing on a single central column is more convenient when a lot of human legs are struggling for space under a cramped table, which explains the popularity of this design in both bars and caravans.

The height of some column tables can be adjusted to adapt them for different tasks, which is a desirable feature. The Kamel table is one such dual-height model, rising from a low coffee table to become a dining table. Others can be fixed in more intermediate positions.

Rounded corners limit injuries in small spaces. Squeezing past the drop-down table on the narrow boat (page 32) would pose a threat to children's heads and adult hips if it had square corners. Moreover, more people can sit in a given area around a circular table than around a rectangular one, another lesson from the bar.

The narrow boat's hinged table doubles as a cupboard door. The high-tech, metal-mesh, wall-mounted table in Eva Jiricna's apartment (page 87) is held by a pair of ball-and-socket joints rather than hinges, swinging down from the wall for dinner parties. Swing-down tables are popular space-savers in caravans, and once again the caravan and camping catalogues are a rich source of space-saving ideas.

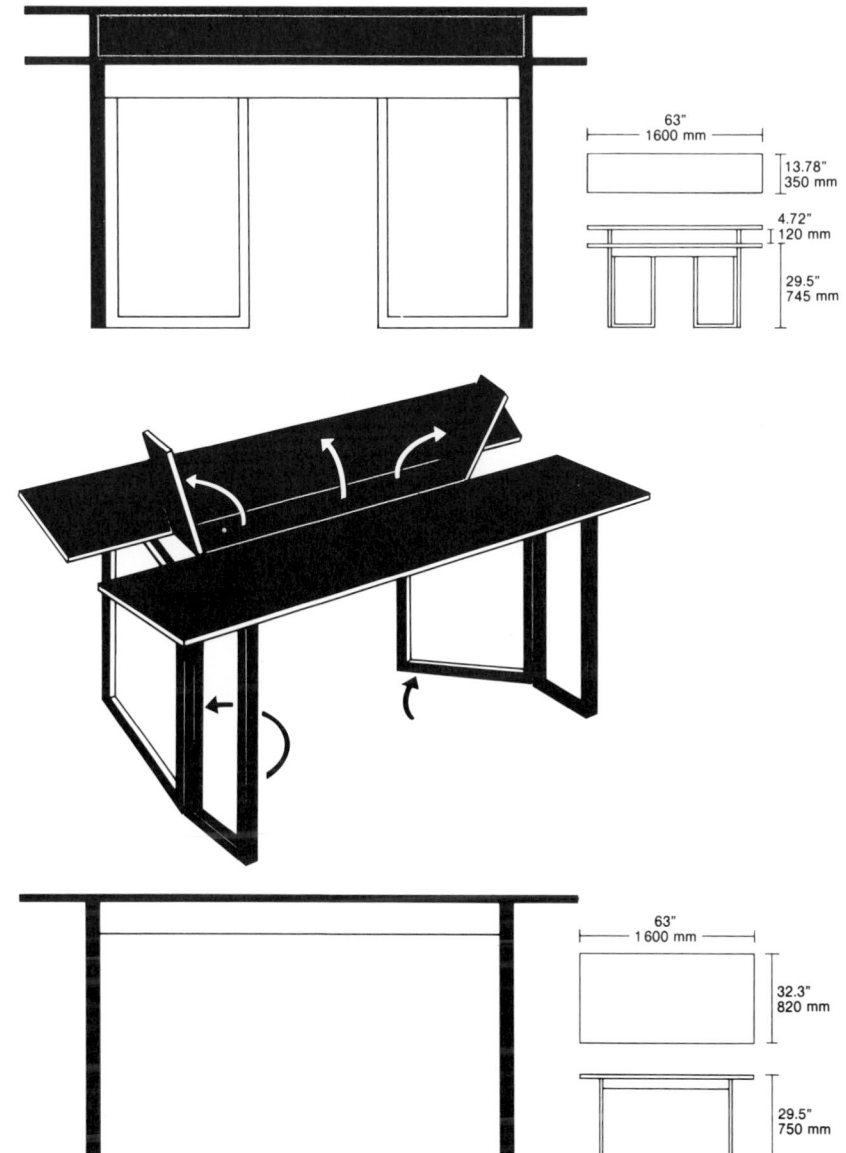

63"
1600 mm

13.78"
350 mm

4.72"
120 mm

29.5"
745 mm

63"
1600 mm

32.3"
820 mm

29.5"
750 mm

The traditional way to change the size of a table is by dropping in a leaf or sliding one out. The French conversion shown here – from side table to dining table – is more dramatic. It gives two kinds of table, not *just two sizes. In small spaces the same table, and the same room are often used for many functions – this piece answers the other problem, of how to turn a sitting-room into a dining-room.*

The exploitation of colour and illusion can make rooms feel larger and brighter. Decoration is one area where custom-made luxury is particularly affordable and practical in a small space. No expensive materials are needed to use the potential of paint, but customising a mansion is clearly a much more demanding project. The major investment in a small space is patience, as small-scale decorative work must, like miniature paintings, be meticulous.

There are well established rules of thumb for painting small rooms. They carry no force of law, and many traditional tiny rooms, such as a narrow boat cabin (see page 32), have successfully flouted the rules for well over a century. Nevertheless, the rules can provide useful guidelines.

They state that:

Cool neutral colours such as oyster, azure or grey make walls seem further away and are therefore known as 'receding' colours.

White ceilings make low rooms feel less oppressive.

Late fifteenth-century inlaid panelling made by the Florentine craftsman Baccio Pontelli (d.1492) for a ducal study. The room was quite small – less than seventeen feet by twelve (5.2 x 3.7m) – but the decoration most lavish. Rich colour and materials, pictorial devices (trompe l'oeil and perspective), and personal references (the study has the Duke's name and mottoes inscribed round the walls) are appropriate to little rooms.

Vertical stripes on a wall make it appear taller, but a prison-like array of well defined stripes can aggravate a feeling of enclosure in small rooms.

Major colour contrasts are to be avoided.

The eye is taken beyond the limits of a little room by painting the window frame in a bright colour.

Patterns should be small and regular.

Patterns should be on a light-coloured background to create a sense of space behind the pattern.

Matt emulsion paint will disguise flaws in a wall, whereas silk or gloss paint emphasise surface texture.

Painting all the appliances and furniture in the room the same colour will reduce visual confusion and make it feel more spacious. This technique can work well in a kitchen, where the cabinets, fridge, washing-machine, dishwasher and cooker can all be repainted. The cooker is the trickiest item, as the surface is subjected to high and sudden heat. The old enamel should be stripped off completely before the cooker is reassembled. This work can be carried out by a car accident-repair shop.

Some effective decorative devices demand neither artistic talent nor paint. The small lavatory in Charles Jencks' London home has a frieze of postcards running around the wall just above the dado. The cards are displayed in simple wooden frames,

Stencilling in a Paris street – the phenomenon of fast production-line graffiti proves just how easy it is to have your own way on your walls.

and they can be changed instantly as they are just slotted into the frame through the small gap between frame-top and wall. Postcard displays can be very self-conscious. A bathroom, for instance, can be covered in postcards showing only sunsets or seascapes.

This multiple use of unlikely materials has often been used by artists and architects. Mies van der Rohe's design for a brewer's display at the Barcelona exhibition, for example, was built around a line of hundreds of identical beer bottles, individually uninteresting but collectively decorative.

The stencil is a simple, traditional method of multiplying a painted image. Although the beginner would be wise to avoid over-ambitious attempts to cover the wall with complex multicoloured imagery, the successful personalization of a room is within the reach of the untrained stenciller.

The great exponents of decoration without training are the largely anonymous army of graffiti artists, who have been spraying their city territory like tomcats in the last decade. Among their major achievements is the complete redesign of the New York Subway livery, but their most refined work covers the walls of Paris, where they use stencils and an aerosol spray for a fast and accurate finish.

In 1985 the Parisian authorities began spraying back, as the *Organisation de Lutte contre Graffiti et Affichages Sauvages* (Organization for the Fight against Graffiti and

Flyposting), known as OLGA, set about wiping off the artworks with a high-pressure spray of air and grit.

The street stencillers cut their images in card or thin metal. Clear acetate sheet is a stable, easily cut and easy-to-clean alternative for home use. Card can grow soggy after repeated paint applications, but it can be waterproofed with a soaking in silicone spray – sold for treating fabric and carpets – followed by a squeeze beween two sheets of newspaper. It is ready for use when the paper soaks up no more greasy marks.

Books of ready-cut stencils rarely contain the image you want, but they can help you work out how a stencil is made. When you have selected an image, draw it on the card, acetate or metal and cut it out with a surgical blade. These are sold by art suppliers. You cut out the areas you want to colour in, which may be the outline of the image or the image itself. If parts drop out due to design flaws or scalpel slips, you can reassemble the stencil using thin strips of masking tape.

Before you cover your wall in stencil images, hang up a test piece of your chosen shape and colour to see if you really want to live with it. One of the great advantages of the stencil is that you can correct all your major errors of drawing and colour before you make any permanent marks on the wall.

During painting, hold the stencil to the wall with low-tack masking tape. This prevents the stencil slipping and lets you lift it from time to time to see how the work is evolving.

Spray paints will drip if over-applied. An alternative is the artist's brush dipped in paint and wiped almost dry on kitchen paper before the stencil is applied. The most suitable paint is gouache/emulsion mixed with indelible ink. Paint from the outside edges towards the centre.

There are other short cuts to transfer an image to the wall, even for such an apparently complex technique as *trompe l'oeil*, which is the drawing of convincing perspective illusions on the walls, furniture, floors or ceilings. Artists and designers have been faking materials and painting illusory spaces for thousands of years. The tradition runs from ancient Egypt – where the temples' stone columns were cut to look like petrified bundles of papyrus – to wood-grain Formica and tile-patterned vinyl flooring. It seems the first thing you do with a new material is make it look like the one it is replacing.

Trompe l'oeil images can be transferred to the wall by the technique dear to painters of large-scale public murals. They divide the wall up into squares, which can be numbered for easy reference, divide the picture up into the same number of squares, and transfer the image square by square. This may appear to be a very childish approach, but Durer woodcuts show that it was used by the most accomplished old masters.

An alternative way of getting the image on the wall is to make a slide of it, project this on to the chosen surface and paint over that. David Hockney has regularly used this device to create his paintings.

It is a fast and easy job to change your room dramatically by draping the walls and ceiling entirely in fabric. No sewing-machine is needed, not even a needle and thread, as this no-sew policy calls for neither hems, seams nor pins. The fabric just hangs loose, draped over a wooden ridge pole fixed across the centre of the room from wall to wall and a rod fixed in the same way to the top of the wall at each side. If you prefer to avoid erecting the poles or would rather the fabric did not hang loose, it can be stapled in position. This is a rapid and easy job with a staple gun.

This technique can look good in cheap ethereal muslin or lining material. It may be possible to buy a secondhand parachute whose 'drop-by' date has passed. The smaller your space, the less it will cost. A covering of fabric is faster and easier than replastering or redecorating bad walls, and you may not wish to decorate for a landlord. Fabric can also be taken with you when you leave.

Fabric makes a room feel very relaxing and it is quite effective at muffling sound. Remember that the wall is still there behind it. It can look nicely peculiar if you start hanging pictures on your 'tent' wall. Low energy lights set between the fabric and the wall can also create interesting effects. Fireproofing the fabric is a sensible precaution. Waterproofing the fabric is not necessary, though swathes of fabric are not a good idea in damp rooms such as kitchens or bathrooms, where it will soak up moisture.

INDEX

INDEX

ACKNOWLEDGEMENTS

Among the many people who contributed to this book I should like to thank the following in particular:

Peter Campbell, partner and friend, with whom I worked out the original concept and who continued to work on every stage of the project. Many of the ideas in this book are his; he wrote part of it; he made many suggestions which are incorporated in the parts I wrote, and he designed it.

Caroline Evans not only researched the photographs for the book but contributed many of the ideas and words. Her knowledge of architecture was invaluable.

Leslie Dick researched both in London and New York.

Margaret Crowther organised sections of the book.

Dieter Klein convinced me – and others – it was possible, and provided crucial support.

Georgina Denison and the staff of Malone Gill Productions believed in the project, made the television series possible and made their material freely available during the writing of the book.

Terry Braun, who directed the television series, was responsible for much of the most interesting material coming to light. He also designed the set shown on the cover.

Liney Li helped immeasurably in the later stages of the book.

Since this is my only opportunity, I should also like to thank the Limehouse crew who worked on 'Space Craft', and who made the experience so enjoyable. In fact I would like to dedicate the book to them.

ILLUSTRATIONS

The illustrations are reproduced by kind permission of the following:
page 2 – Architectural Association, London; page 3 – Taisuke Ogawa/'The Japan Architect'; page 6 – Geoff Howard; page 7 – Collection 'Air France'; page 8 – Mike Abrahams/Network (top); Malone Gill Productions (bottom); page 9 – The Boeing Company (bottom); page 10 – Mary Evans Picture Library; page 11 – Sheila Rock; page 12 – Mark Swenarton (top); Louis Hellman (bottom); page 14 – 'Architectural Review' (top); National Trust for Scotland (bottom); page 17 – Royal Photographic Society; page 19 – Taisuke Ogawa/'The Japan Architect';

page 20 – Shakertown at Pleasant Hill, Inc.; page 21 – Shakertown, South Union (left); Shakertown at Pleasant Hill Inc. (right); page 22 Masao Arai/'The Japan Architect'; page 25 – The National Trust; page 26 – 'The New York Times'; page 29 – Prof. Margaret Harker/The Trustees of Sir John Soane's Museum; page 31 – Architectural Association, London; page 32 – The Waterways Museum, Stoke Bruerne (top); the drawing is an adaptation of a drawing by John M. Hill, whose help we would like to acknowledge; page 33 – Geoff Howard; page 34 – Geoff Howard; page 36 – Horniman Museum, London; page 37 – NASA (top); Mary Evans Picture Library (bottom); page 39 – 'Illegal Facades' by Jerzy Wojtowicz (left); Barnaby's Picture Library (right); page 40 – Martin Charles/'Architectural Review'; page 41 - Gerald Duckworth and Co. Ltd; page 42 – 'Architectural Review' (left); Castilia spa/Aram Designs Ltd (right); page 46 – Hunterian Art Gallery, University of Glasgow; page 47 – Manfred Wolff-Plottegg; page 48 – The Trustees of Sir John Soane's Museum; page 49 – 'Perspective' by Jan Vredeman de Vries (Dover Publications, New York); page 50 – Alessandro Ferrari (architect)/'Abitare'; page 51 – Oberto Gili (photographer)/Hawkinson and Smith-Miller (architects); page 52 – Oberto Gili (photographer)/Hawkinson and Smith-Miller (architects); page 53 – Cobuild Design, New York; page 54 – Preservation Associates of Savannah, Georgia; page 55 – Architectural Press; page 56 – Architectural Press; page 57 – John Wildgoose/Guardian Newspapers Ltd; page 60 – Bristol Energy Centre; page 62 – Gerald Duckworth and Co. Ltd; page 64 – Michael Holford; page 65 – The Wharton Esherick Museum; page 67 – Velux; page 69 – Jean Kallina; page 70 – Toni d'Urso/'Abitare'; page 71 Ron Arad/One Off Ltd; page 73 – Bisque, London; page 74 – Imperial War Museum, London; page 78 – Ulster Folk and Transport Museum; page 79 – Barnaby's Picture Library; page 80 – 'Yorkshire Post' (left); John Michael Vlach/University of Georgia Press (right); page 82 – Paul Overy; page 83 – G.B.A. Williams (architect); page 84 – Royal Photographic Society (left); 'Architectural Review' (right); page 85 –

Marco de Valdivia (photograph)/Hawkinson and Smith-Miller (architects); page 86– Hawkinson and Smith-Miller Architects; page 87 – Richard Bryant/Arcaid; page 88 – Richard Bryant/Arcaid; page 90 – Eva Jiricna (architect); page 92 - Geoff Howard; page 93 – Jean Kallina; page 95 – Alessandro Ferrari (architect)/'Abitare'; page 96 – Toni d'Urso (photographer)/'Abitare'; page 97 – Toni d'Urso (photographer)/'Abitare'; page 98 – Malone Gill Productions; page 99 – Her Majesty's Stationery Office; page 100 – The National Trust (top); Richard Bryant/Arcaid (bottom); page 101 – Bosch; page 102 – Smallbone of Devizes (left); Electrolux (centre); Berry Magicoal Ltd (right); page 103 – King Mini-Kitchen (left); Anthony Byers / Electricity Council (centre); C. P. Hart (right); page 105 – Dana Levy; page 106 – Manfred Wolff-Plottegg; page 107 – Her Majesty's Stationery Office; page 108 – Heaton's Bathrooms Ltd (top); Robert H. Harvey/Compact Bathrooms (bottom); page 109 – Tefal (bottom); page 111 – Home House Society Trustees, Courtauld Institute Galleries, London. Princes Gate Collection; page 114 – Jan Staller (photographer) /Richard H. Lewis (architect); page 115 – Faust Talbot/Siematic; page 116 – Louis Vuitton S.A.; page 117 – Louis Vuitton S.A.; page 118 – Campmor; page 119 – Sony (UK) Ltd; page 120 – Pierre Botschi; page 121 –'Architectural Review'; page 122 – Louis Vuitton S.A.; page 123 – Futon Company, London (top); The Space-Saving Bed Centre, London (bottom); page 124 – Ron Arad/One Off Ltd (left); Murphy Door Bed Co. Inc. (right); page 126 – Pira Ltd (left); The American Museum in Britain, Bath (top right); Balans / Wiltshier Contract Furnishing Ltd (bottom right); page 127 – Pira Ltd (top left); Balans/Wiltshier Contract Furnishing Ltd (bottom left); by courtesy of the Board of Trustees of the Victoria and Albert Museum, London (top centre); Pira Ltd (bottom centre); Seccose/Ideas for Living (right); page 129 – VIA, Paris; page 130 – The Metropolitan Museum of Art, Rogers Fund, 1939.

The drawings on pages 27, 32, 58–59, 61, 63, 70, and 72 are by Alison George.